GOT *Issues* MUCH?

Celebrities Share Their Traumas and Triumphs

By Randi Reisfeld and Marie Morreale

SCHOLASTIC INC.
New York   Toronto   London   Auckland   Sydney
Mexico City   New Delhi   Hong Kong

Pages 202–203 from *Little Girl Lost* by Drew Barrymore with Todd Gold. Copyright © 1990 by Drew Barrymore. Published by Pocket Books, a division of Simon and Schuster, Inc.
Pages 216–222 from *Michelle Kwan: My Story, Heart of a Champion.* Copyright © 1997 by Michelle Kwan Corp. Reprinted by permission of Scholastic Inc.
"Puff Daddy" by Mikal Gilmore. From ROLLING STONE, August 7, 1997. "Puff Daddy: I've Risen from the Dead a Couple of Times" by Anthony Bozza. From ROLLING STONE, December 25, 1997–January 8, 1998. By Straight Arrow Publishers Company, L.P. 1997. All rights reserved. Reprinted by permission.

Cover, clockwise from top left: Brandy — Nina Prommer/Globe Photos; Jennifer Love Hewitt — Fitzroy Barrett/Globe Photos; James Van Der Beek — Dorothy Low/Shooting Star; Sarah Michelle Gellar — Lisa Rose/Globe Photos; Neve Campbell — Greg Vie/Globe Photos; Nick Carter — Larry Busacca/Retna Limited; Michelle Williams — Terry Lilly/Gamma Liaison; Nicholas Brendon — Lisa Rose/Globe Photos; Usher — Fitzroy Barrett/Globe Photos; Joshua Jackson — Dorothy Low/Shooting Star; Melissa Joan Hart — Lisa Rose/Globe Photos; Leonardo DiCaprio — Yoram Kahana/Shooting Star; Taylor Hanson — Pierre Paul Poulin/Sygma; Katie Holmes — Dorothy Low/Shooting Star; page 3: Lisa Rose/Globe Photos; 12: Barry King/Shooting Star; 22: Roger Karnbad/Celebrity Photo; 28: Miranda Shen/Celebrity Photo; 34: Larry Busacca/Retna Limited; 41: Gregory Pace/Sygma; 46: Lisa Rose/Globe Photos; 52: Lisa Rose/Globe Photos; 57: Fitzroy Barrett/Globe Photos; 62: Miranda Shen/Celebrity Photo; 70: Janet Gough/Celebrity Photo; 74: Lisa Rose/Globe Photos; 85: Ron Davis/Shooting Star; 92: Courtesy of Elle Productions; 96: Pacha/Corbis; 101: Jeff Slocomb/Outline Press; 107: Barry King/Shooting Star; 117: Gregory Pace/Sygma; 124: Courtesy of LaFace Records; 129: Courtesy of Arista; 134: Kevin Winter/Celebrity Photo; 149: Theo Kingma/Shooting Star; 155: Larry Busacca/Retna Limited; 161: Gilbert Flores/Celebrity Photo; 165: Anthony Cutajar; 169: Anthony Cutajar/London Features Int'l; 181: Paul Fenton/Shooting Star; 189, left: Roman Salicki/Shooting Star; 189, right: Roman Salicki/Shooting Star; 193: Barry King/Shooting Star; 201: Ron Davis/Shooting Star; 209: Derrick Santini/ESP; 215: J. Barry Mittan, Tallahassee, FL; 223: Barry King/Shooting Star.

Interior design by Louise Bova

ISBN 0-590-63274-4

12 11 10 9 8 7 6 5 4 3 2   9/9 0 1 2 3 4/0

Printed in the U.S.A.

First Scholastic printing, March 1999

ACKNOWLEDGMENTS

This is a book we've long wanted to write. As former editorial directors of teen magazines (*16* and *Teen Machine,* respectively), we've interviewed and gotten to know thousands of young celebrities over the years. We've often found their true-life stories incredibly poignant and ultimately more interesting than any movie, TV show, or song they've been involved with. We've always sensed that those stories could be inspiring to their young fans — if only there were a place to hear them.

This, we hope, is that place.

We sincerely thank those representatives of celebrities who helped us, and of course, the stars themselves who graciously participated.

Yet this book could not have been written without the help, support, and vision of many other people. These are the people who gave it the green light — who came up with cool ideas, who designed it, produced it, and (oops, our bad) forgave its tardiness!

Most are on the Scholastic team, a team we're proud to be part of. In random order, they are: Jean Feiwel, Craig Walker, Eleanor Berger, Bethany Buck, Francesca Massari, Madalina Stefan, Mark Seidenfeld, David Levithan, Helen Perelman, Jessica Kaplan, Nancy Smith, Louise Bova, Samantha Kish, Maria Barbo, David Goddy, Emily Sachar, plus, always, Fran Lebowitz and Jason Weinstein of Writers House.

On a very personal note, Marie would like to thank her brother William V. Morreale, who solved a twenty-five-year issue . . . with love.

On the homefront, we bow at the altar of our friends, families, and pets — with whom we *never* have issues (yeah, right). Only kidding. Thanks to all.

— Randi Reisfeld and Marie Morreale

TABLE OF CONTENTS

Relationship Issues

4 Family Issues

5 Money, School, and Health Issues

6 Issues of Loss

7 Issues of Disappointment and Defeat

INTRODUCTION

So . . . what *are* issues exactly?

Some people call them problems, or traumas, angst, or emotional hurdles. Issues are your real life deals. Doesn't matter what you call them, they come calling on you, no matter who you are.

Issues are the stuff you're bugged about. They can be annoying and nasty but temporary, or they can be huge and seemingly never ending. Sometimes they seem insurmountable. Reality: when you're going through them, they're the worst.

There are all kinds of issues. They can be about friendship, family, relationships, body image and self-esteem, money, school, health, loss, and disappointment, to name a few.

Issues can be anything from your best friend bailing on you for another friend, to the kids at school making fun of you.

They can be everything from sibling rivalry, to the conflicting emotions when parents get divorced.

They're the problems of having no money when everyone else seems to — to the pain of just being different, not fitting in. Got a charter membership in the "I've Been Dumped Club?" It hurts — big time.

When you're dealing with your issues, it can seem like no one *gets it* — no one understands, even if they say they do.

Of course, the people who care — parents, teachers, guidance counselors, clergy — tell you what's meant to make you feel better. Things like: *time heals all wounds, you'll get over it;* to *she's not worth having as a friend; it's not your fault; just be true to yourself and it'll all work out.* All of it is said with the best of intentions, and most of it is wise and true.

But here's a group of people maybe you *haven't* heard from, the people who supposedly have it all: the looks, the talent, the money, the hip-cred. They're today's top young stars, the rockers and actors we admire. They're the people we look at and say, "If only I could trade lives with him or her, all my issues would disappear."

Or not.

Because nearly all of them have been there, done that. All have had and even now, have major issues.

Within the pages of this book you'll find the stories you haven't heard before. You'll learn how Leonardo felt when kids dissed him; how Backstreet Boy Nick Carter felt when he had no friends; how much Neve Campbell hurt when all the boys at school said she was ugly; how Jennifer Love Hewitt was uncomfortable with her body; how Sarah Michelle Gellar didn't kick butt when she got left out at school.

Issues. You've got 'em? Join the human race. We all do. Want to hear the real celebrity deal? Turn the page.

SARAH MICHELLE GELLAR

1

NEVE CAMPBELL

FRIENDSHIP ISSUES

BRANDY

MICHELLE WILLIAMS

SETH GREEN

NICK CARTER

MELISSA JOAN HART

LEANN RIMES

"You've *got* to have friends," right? Friendship is sooo important — who'd argue with that?

Friends are everything. They're people you can tell anything to, do fun stuff with, laugh at the same jokes with, who understand what you're going through, 'cause they're going through it, too. Friends get it.

Friends are honest with each other, friends can trust each other, friends listen. And above all, friends are supportive — "knowing you can always count on me," as the famous song about friendship says.

Everyone wants friends. If you've got lots of them, you're proclaimed popular. If you've got one or two close buds, you feel part of a posse.

But when you've got no friends, it's outsider time. You feel like a loser. And that hurts. Yet that's exactly what some of your favorite stars went through, not so long ago.

Here's what they dealt with and how they made it through — and lived to tell about it.

SARAH MICHELLE GELLAR

Sarah Michelle Gellar is a huge star. She's beautiful, talented, and admired much. The petite powerhouse stars in a megahit series, *Buffy the Vampire Slayer,* and in box office bonanza movies, including *I Know What You Did Last Summer* and *Scream 2.* Sarah the star is sought after as a magazine cover girl; reporters hang on her every quote; fan-run cybershrines abound.

In private, Sarah the person is nurturing, generous, gregarious. She's gracious to fans, a protective "mom" to her pet pooch. She counts many people as close friends and enjoys a tight relationship with her family.

Bottom line? Here on earth, *and* out there in the showbiz stratosphere, Sarah rocks. She is the slayer — she is the Buffster! What's not to admire — what's not to like? Funny you should ask.

Life wasn't always quite so kickin' for Sarah. School days are remembered as cruel days, a time when friends were few and far between. There are lots of reasons.

Sarah started acting professionally at four years old when she got discovered by a talent agent. Soon after, she nabbed her first role in a TV movie.

By the age of five, she was Burger King's official spokeskid, the star of more than thirty nationally televised commercials.

By nine, she was a pro on Broadway, acting alongside Matthew Broderick and Eric Stoltz in the play *The Widow Claire*.

At fourteen, she starred in the first-ever daytime serial for teens, *Swan's Crossing*.

From ages fifteen through eighteen, she costarred in the most-watched soap opera on TV, *All My Children*.

At seventeen, she was nominated for a Daytime Emmy Award.

In 1995, at the age of eighteen, she *won* a Daytime Emmy!

Has Sarah Michelle Gellar achieved showbiz success much? To the max. Every bit of it cost her during her school years.

"I was always excluded from everything."

Because Sarah has been in the public eye for so many years, she's been longtime interview bait. While she's notoriously private today, she wasn't always so guarded. She used to talk freely, mainly about her career, which she loves, but also about her life off camera — parts of which she did so *not* love.

The tough times started in elementary school. An only child who grew up in a single-parent home on New York's Upper East Side, Sarah attended an exclusive private school called Columbia Grammar and Preparatory. There, she not only felt different, she felt shunned. For starters, unlike many of her classmates, Sarah was not wealthy.

As she candidly confided in a soap magazine, "I had a hard time, because I didn't like the kids. I didn't have anything in common with them. Many of those students were used to having everything handed to them on a silver platter. Everything *I* got, I worked hard for and got on my own. And kids were hard on me."

Perhaps Sarah might have eventually overcome those early feelings of resentment, but she was never around long enough to warm up to the other kids or give them time to get to know her. As she explained, "After school and on the weekends, I had to choose between going out with all the kids or going on auditions."

Because Sarah loved — really loved — acting, the latter won out, nearly every single time. It was her undoing with her peers. "The second you start missing school and social events, you stop getting invited to parties, and people stop talking to you," she once said. In a *TV Guide* interview, she added, "I was always excluded from everything because I was different. That's difficult when you're a child."

While Sarah hasn't copped to being an exiled "lonely only," in so many words, she has admitted that as a kid and young teenager, she spent many hours parked in front of the TV set, watching afternoon soap operas. And while Sarah is justifiably proud of all her extracurricular activities, none were team sports or clubs where she might have found a circle of friends. Instead, she took private lessons in tae kwon do and figure skating. She excelled in both.

"Junior high school was a hurtful time."

Things got worse in junior high school. Admittedly a tough time for most 'tweens and teens, junior high was its own little horror show for the girl who'd one day be the Slayer. Completely without irony, Sarah's declared, "Junior high school was my *Buffy* experience. I hated it. I was not popular to the extreme. I was the girl nobody liked, who was weird and quirky. I felt different and awkward."

By that time, Sarah had quite an impressive acting résumé. She'd been in more than a hundred commercials and had done roles in TV shows such as the popular Robert Urich starrer, *Spenser: For Hire*, and several TV movies, and had even acted in a Broadway play opposite Matthew Broderick and Eric Stoltz.

By seventh grade — this was 1990, way before it was cool — she wore a pager to school so she could be contacted at all times, in case she was needed to go to an audition or fly off at a moment's notice for an acting gig.

It all sounds like a glam life for a young teen. And in many respects it really was. Sarah got to travel to exotic places. She got to hang with big stars, eat at fancy restaurants, wear cool clothes.

What she couldn't do was share that excitement. Not with her classmates, anyway. She confessed in an interview, "I went through a tough time in seventh and eighth grades. If I talked about what I did — my acting jobs — I was labeled a snob. And if I didn't talk about it, I was also labeled a snob, obnoxious. It was a no-win situation. And the kids gave me such a hard time. Back then, I didn't understand why."

Sarah's mom and other adults tried explaining. "They'd say, 'They're jealous of you.' I couldn't figure out what they had to be jealous *of*! These were very wealthy kids who had beautiful clothes and houses. They didn't have to do anything to earn any of this stuff — I worked for everything I had. Now, of course, when I look back, I realize those kids were jealous of what I had done, but at the time I didn't understand it, and it was so hurtful."

Sarah claims she did make some stabs at assimilation, but perhaps because they were halfhearted, they didn't work out. "I tried to be a jock. I tried to be cool. But I guess that was my time to feel I didn't know where I fit in. I couldn't find my place," she has admitted.

The turning point: Switching schools

Sarah began high school in 1992, and that's when things started to change for her. Not, right away, for the better. She'd started ninth grade at LaGuardia High School for the Performing Arts, where she again found herself odd girl out. Although there were other talented kids in the student body, most were honing their skills, not actually working like Sarah. "And it didn't help that I was a nerd," she noted to the on-line Mr. Showbiz. "I was very into my studies."

That was the year she experimented with her look — much. "I went through this crazy phase," she mentioned in *People* magazine. "I would dye my hair a different color every week. I wanted to be a really goth teenager." But if that was a bid for popularity, it didn't work.

Instead, Sarah got more into her work, nailing her first role in a series. *Swan's Crossing*, which lasted only a season, was the first daily daytime soap for teens.

Finally, at the end of ninth grade, Sarah's mom made a suggestion. She encouraged her daughter to switch schools. And that made a huge difference.

In tenth grade, Sarah enrolled in New York City's Professional Children's School. Among its former students are Christina Ricci and Macaulay Culkin. There, finally, Sarah Michelle Gellar found acceptance . . . and friends.

"It's an amazing place," Sarah gushed in an on-line interview. "I love it. It's for anyone with irregular schedules — kids who are musicians from the Juilliard School of Music, ballerinas from the School of American Ballet, and writers. Just the most talented group of young people. The kids are incredible! There's someone off playing the cello or the violin — and there's someone here who left home at the age of four to go to the School of American Ballet. There are people from all over the world, and they're all very supportive. They understand the rejection we go through in this business. Someone will say, 'You know, I was up to the last cut for the San Francisco Conservatory, and I didn't make it.'"

But it wasn't just the understanding of work pressures that made Sarah love being at that school. It was the social aspect, too. "Everyone is respected," she detailed. "If somebody doesn't like you, they simply don't talk to you. They don't make fun of you or punish you. You can mess around with how you dress. You really have that chance to find yourself, and I thank God for that school. It was my lifeline." Her best friends there were a fencer and a ballerina.

In one of her first interviews for *Buffy*, she reflected further on her experience there. "I think high school scares everyone. I think that no matter how popular you are, or how unpopular, high school is a scary place."

Even at the Professional Children's School, Sarah contends she wasn't cool. "I was more Willow than Buffy," she insists. Mostly, it was because, as usual, she wasn't there a lot. And her choices remained static. "I had to decide between going to my junior prom and going to the Emmys," she mentioned to a reporter. "I went to the Emmys, but at least I got to go to the afterprom party."

She learned something else from finally being able to participate in school stuff: She didn't even like it all that much. As she admitted to a reporter, "At [the Professional Children's School] I do have it all. I go to proms and I go to formals, and you know what? I yawn at them!"

The timing of Sarah's school switch couldn't have been more perfect. After *Swan's Crossing* ended, she began her highly publicized three-year stint at *All My Children*. And while she loved the school, achieving a balance between acting five days a week and schoolwork was a challenge. She noted, "Most actors just go home after work and learn their lines for the next day. I'd go home, do geometry, algebra, and all my other subjects — then memorize the script and learn my lines."

Be that as it may, Sarah only spent two and a half years in high school. Not because she dropped out. She simply — well, not so simply — worked double time and completed two years in one. By 1994, she'd earned her diploma.

Looking back: Issues remain

Five years beyond high school, Sarah is able to look back and, if not exactly smile, at least understand why she made the choices she made — and the reactions of her peers — a little better.

She mused in an interview, "I was not meant to be in Little League or the local ballet school. And I hate it when people say, 'You missed your childhood.' Childhood can be awful. Kids can be so petty, especially girls. I was lucky to miss a lot of that. So yes, there were times when I'd miss a sleepover, but big deal! Instead of being at a sleepover, I was at a party at Sardi's for a Broadway show with Matthew Broderick and Eric Stoltz. So look what I gained!"

Working with adults taught her other lessons as well. As Sarah gamely ran down for a reporter: "I learned how to talk to people, how to be social, things that a lot of kids don't know. I've found that kids in high school are often clones of each other, but this — being an actress — gave me an individual personality. A lot of kids go through college and try to find themselves, but I *know* who I am. I've learned what's *not* important. Everything I have, I worked for. And everything I've earned I can honestly say I deserved because I've worked so hard for it."

Interestingly, now that Sarah's officially in the grown-up world (she turned twenty-two in April 1999), she really hasn't changed much at all. Work — these days as the Buffster *and* A-list movie star — still comes first. She recently declared, "I'm a workaholic and proud of it." As for a social life? "My job is my significant other," she half joked.

What has changed is that now she finally *does* fit in. She has friends much. Most are fellow actors. To them, Sarah is loved as nurturer, adviser, mother hen. She's always there when someone's sick, as *Buffy* co-star Alyson Hannigan has told, and by all accounts, is unfailingly thoughtful and generous with gifts. She lets her friends know she cares.

Those friends treat her in kind. When Freddie Prinze, Jr., with whom she costarred in *I Know What You Did Last Summer*, noticed that she was getting too skinny, he came over to her house and cooked dinner.

Clearly, many of the friends Sarah has made *are* fellow actors.

They understand all the personal rejection she went through during her school years. In a national magazine, Sarah recounted conversations with actress Rebecca Gayheart. "No one would talk to her at school because she was this girl from Kentucky with pigtails," Sarah said of Rebecca. Jerry O'Connell (*Scream 2*) sympathized with Sarah "because he was the fat kid from *Stand By Me*."

If her friends are mostly her age these days, there's still one place in her life where she remains more comfortable around folks who are older. That's the dating scene. "I don't have much in common with [boys] my own age," she told *Rolling Stone* in a famous cover story. "So I always date people who are older. A guy who's twenty-two, he's in college and is kind of finding himself . . . and that's not me."

Looking back on her own experience, tough as it sometimes was, Sarah would probably not do anything differently. She says, "Your childhood is what you make it. If you want [something], go get it, because you only have one life to live."

Finally, she's totally happy with the one she's living.

NEVE CAMPBELL

Neve Campbell — *she* has issues? Neve-*r*! Well, it's hard to imagine she does — or ever did. Right now, the dreamy, coltish, confidence-oozing Canadian is pretty much sitting on top of the showbiz world.

Playing vulnerable, complex Julia Salinger on *Party of Five* became her launching pad to movie stardom. In the past three years, Neve has starred in *six* big screeners — uh, make that *Scream*-ers. It started with *The Craft*, after which she became famous stalkee Sidney Prescott in the box office smashes *Scream* and *Scream 2*. Those led to top billing in *Wild Things*, *54*, and *Three to Tango*.

She's admired for her talent — well compensated for it, too; heralded for her beauty (can you say *People* magazine's 50 Most Beautiful?); and looked up to by millions of fans. In the real world, Neve shares extreme closeness with her brother and a tight circle of friends. So, yeah, she does have it all.

And issues, too.

Take a closer look — and listen. The roles Neve has become

most famous for — *Po5*'s Julia and *Scream*'s Sidney — are characters who are often confused, scared, vulnerable. Check it: Neve
plays insecure well. Could be because she's been there, done that.
"She's a fragile soul," say those who know her best.

Actor Christian Campbell, Neve's older brother and closest kin,
said this to *US* magazine and to *Rolling Stone*: "It's difficult for people to tell [how insecure she is, because] she gives off this, 'It's all
right, I'm confident with myself' kind of thing. She holds [all her
real emotions] in. That's her strength — but it's also her weakness.
It makes her sort of hard to get to."

Neve doesn't deny it. In many of her in-depth interviews, she's
candidly revealed a childhood that was so emotionally grueling,
she suffered a breakdown at the age of fourteen. Here's what Neve
has said about the tough stuff, how she got through it all, and what
issues linger still.

Friends? "No one would spend five cents to send me a cookie."

Neve Campbell was born on October 3, 1973, in Guelph, a
town outside Toronto, Canada. If she ever had self-confidence or
felt attractive, she hasn't said. Instead, she remembers feeling quite
the opposite. "I was pretty geeky," she told *US* magazine. "I was really skinny and had huge feet and knobby knees." Early photos of
the star show a tot squinting at the camera, seemingly uncertain of
whether to smile or not.

Worse than feeling that way about herself was the negative rein-
forcement she got from other kids. In a revealing *TV Guide* profile,
Neve recalled a self-esteem low point. She was only nine years old,
a time when most kids have at least one friend.

"We had this awful thing at school where we had cookies on Valentine's Day. Every student could buy them and send them to other class members. They would call up each student every time [his or her] name came out of the box — meaning someone had bought a cookie for that person.

"I wasn't called up at all. Wait . . . I was called up one time because the *teacher* gave me a cookie. I was devastated. No one would spend five cents to send me a cookie."

She wouldn't cry, refusing to show her humiliation. "I didn't cry a lot when I was a kid," she explained later. "I held a lot in."

She didn't show her emotions at home, either. There her life was anything but normal, anything but solid. Which did little to counter the emotional beating she got at school. "I was very insecure . . . because I didn't have a totally stable home life," she has said.

Her parents, drama teacher Gerry Campbell and dinner theater owner Marnie Neve, divorced when Neve was a baby. The pair subsequently remarried and divorced several times. Neve and Christian lived with their dad. While she loved him, of course, she admitted that opening up about her deepest emotions didn't feel like an option. "You can't talk about everything with your father," she conceded. "There are certain things you can relate only to your mother." What made that close to impossible, in spite of Neve seeing her mom every other weekend, was that her parents rarely spoke to each other.

So Neve not only learned to hold things in, she learned to grow up fast. "When you don't have real solid family, you kind of have to take care of yourself," she noted to reporters, adding, "my childhood was basically nil." That separated her from other kids. "I had a hard time relating to people my own age. I don't know, [stuff like] jokes just to be giddy didn't make a lot of sense to me."

Despite her low self-esteem and lack of friends, little Neve did have a dream. "My father took me to see *The Nutcracker* when I was six. Becoming a ballet dancer became my dream." It also became her dad's dream for her. A mixed blessing, to say the least.

Neve has candidly admitted — time and again — that she was pushed by her dad. As in, "He was very wonderful in that he really pushed me in this business. He pushed my brother also. Both my parents were actors and got married at such a young age and had us at such young ages and didn't get to finish their careers. In a sense, maybe they're living through what we're doing, in a positive way."

Another time, she added, "My father really believed in my brother and me. Sometimes it was hard, because he pushed us when we wanted to quit — but that's okay, because I wouldn't be where I am now."

No question Neve believes that. But the pressure back then was almost unbearable. And it didn't only come from home.

"I was definitely . . . the loser of my class."

Neve started dancing lessons at six, and at the age of nine she was accepted to Toronto's prestigious National Ballet School. There, one hundred twenty-five students got their academic education while enduring rigorous training in dance. "The school was about discipline," Neve has told. "We practiced three to five hours a day." It was a place where everyone shared a common passion. So you'd think friendships might easily blossom. They did — alongside fierce competition.

The goal, for all the kids enrolled, was to get into the National Ballet of Canada. Not everyone would, of course. And for some kids, that made being there a really tough deal. "I can't say I hated the school," Neve told *Sassy*, "but the pressure! We were all competing for the same goal." Each year, the students were evaluated, a time Neve always dreaded. In *USA Today*, she bluntly admitted, "Every year, you're told whether you're going to be kicked out. I pretty much had a nervous breakdown at fourteen."

The pressure, which Neve has categorized as backstabbing, *was* intense — but what made it truly unbearable was another kind of pressure. That's the kind that exists in every school, in every country, at every level: the pressure to be popular. In Neve's mind, she failed miserably at that. Looking back, she attributes her feelings of alienation to her serious nature and the fact that unlike most of the kids there, she wasn't rich. And this: She claims she didn't dress like the other kids. "I was a tomboy when I was a teenager and didn't wear dresses at all." And in the early eighties, she adopted a punk look, which didn't sit well at school. "At the National Ballet School, you had to have your hair up in a bun. I shaved the back of my head, so I had the bun on top of a shaved head. That was my rebellion." At least it was better than the hairdo she had a few years earlier. "At thirteen, I got a perm that made me look like Bozo the Clown."

As she told *Sassy*, "I didn't have a good time at school. I didn't fit in. I was definitely, like, the loser of my class. I was really unpopular — I had absolutely no friends." And it hurt. Much. "I was always in need, in need of love, in need of my family and friends — in need of being accepted." Hope sprung eternal, for the last one. "I would try, like any kid, desperately every moment, thinking, 'Oh, they smiled at me. Wait, maybe they do like me!'"

Neve's hopes were more often dashed than realized. In more than one interview, she has revealed what was no doubt her most devastating moment at the National Ballet School. The boys wrote a song about all the girls in the class, ranking them from prettiest to ugliest. The *last* verse, "Neve-aagh! Neve-aagh!" was reserved for her. "It was about how ugly I was," she said. Now, we have a name for that: harassment. Back then, it was Neve's private pain. That — and the pressure of competing, the pressure she felt at home, the pressure she put on herself — led to what Neve has called a breakdown.

"I got to a place at that school where I hated dance, that was really tragic for me. I had no friends, I didn't fit it, and I was living in residence. When you live with the people you don't fit in with, you're in trouble."

And that led her to quit the school.

"At fourteen," she told *Rolling Stone*, "I kind of had a nervous breakdown and quit. No one ever quit [that school]. It's a fantastic school, training-wise, but they also had, like, seven psychiatrists on staff with only a hundred twenty-five students." In *Sassy*, she added, "It made me hate dancing. And I didn't want to hate dancing."

Neve didn't just quit the National Ballet School, she also quit living at home that year. Instead, she moved in with her brother, Christian, and in tenth grade enrolled in the school he attended. The Claude Watson School for the Arts was an alternative school that offered flexible schedules for artists, actors, and athletes. The pressure to excel at dance and the backstabbing competition were finally over — but sadly, it didn't end up being the panacea she'd been hoping for. Neve was no happier. After a year, she quit school altogether. She'd longed to go to a school where she felt normal, but all she felt there was a huge emotional hole where dance used to be.

Upshot: She was nowhere. The dream to be a dancer appeared to be all but dead. She had an unfinished education, no friends, and no answer to the question, "What do you want to be when you grow up?" She was fifteen.

The turning point: The best years of my life

How Neve got from that low point to where she is now is really pretty simple. You could say it was a twist of fate, but the truth is, she followed her heart. Her issues followed her, too — but this time, she didn't let them stop her.

"When I quit the school, I thought I would never dance again," she explained in several interviews. "But I ran into some other dancers who talked me into auditioning for the Canadian company of the play *Phantom of the Opera*. It was the first big Broadway production in Canada in a long time, a very big deal. I just went along for the experience. There were, like, three hundred girls at this cattle-call audition, and I was so nervous that when they called me, I ran off to the dressing room, bawling my eyes out. [But] some other dancers convinced me to go ahead with it anyway, so I did — and they kept calling me in again and again all day long. Everyone got cut but eight of us. I ended up in the ballet chorus and then I got the part of the Degas Girl. I did that for two years. The next youngest person in the cast was twenty-four — I was fifteen, the youngest ever to do *Phantom* anywhere in the world. So I ended up performing with dancers from the National Ballet of Canada after all. Funny how things work out."

Amazing, really. Neve danced in the *Phantom* chorus for two years — all told, she was in eight hundred performances. It was, up till then, the best time of her life. That's when it all came together. She was doing what she loved and making actual friends among the other dancers, who were no longer competition but peers, in spite of the age difference. A serious boyfriend entered her life at that time, too. It was all good. Finally.

And it only got better. In the audience one night was a theatrical agent, who signed her up. And that's how Neve's acting career was born. She nabbed, first, a role in the short-lived Canadian series called *Catwalk*, in which she played Daisy, a singer and dance teacher. Then she began to win guest-star roles in Canadian-produced TV shows like *Kids in the Hall*, *Are You Afraid of the Dark?*, and *My Secret Identity*. The latter starred starred Jerry O'Connell, who'd later be Neve's boyfriend in *Scream 2*.

After nailing a juicy part in the NBC movie *I Know My Son Is Alive*, she moved to Los Angeles for good. More parts and, even better, *acclaim* followed. She won the Family Film Award as Outstanding Actress in a TV Film for her work in *The Canterville Ghost*, with Patrick Stewart. And then, of course, she became the life of the *Party*, and all the movie roles followed.

Issues still: Who loves ya, baby?

Neve Campbell is a big star now, but like everyone else, she still has issues. They're not so very different from the ones she always had. There are family issues. When she got married a few years ago (she's since divorced), she did not invite her family to her wedding. She explained to *TV Guide*, "I love my family very much, and that was obviously a difficult decision. My immediate family, they're all incredible — but not in the same room, you know?"

There are emotional issues. "I still don't cry a lot," she has confessed.

And always, friendship issues. "I don't want to put up barriers," she told the *New York Post*, "but I find myself in circumstances where some people want to be your friend because of who you are [a star], instead of who you are *inside*. It's hard to believe that a job can cause that to happen, but it does."

The difference now is, Neve has learned to deal with her issues, to tease out the positive stuff, and to trash what's purely negative.

As she told *All About You!* magazine, "I really don't believe that anything is negative. Any experience, if you learn from it, you've made it positive somehow."

There's little doubt how Neve has turned the traumas of her growing-up years into a positive — she uses all those feelings in her acting. "As long as I touch people through my acting, nothing else matters," she asserts. And she touches them through her very convincing acting. Often, she has felt what her characters feel.

She's almost able to shrug off the early hurt and not let it affect her friendships now. "I'd rather not live my life distrusting — it's better to live your life openly, and if I get hurt, I get hurt. Learn your lesson and move on."

Neve has also learned to use her celebrity — which can be privacy-robbing and off-putting — in a positive way. One of her half sibs, Damian, suffers from the neurological disorder called Tourette's Syndrome, which causes involuntary tics and vocalizations. Neve has signed on as National Youth Spokesperson for the

Tourette's Syndrome Association. "Educating the public about it is very important to me," she asserts.

People listen to her because she's a star — and she's a star, partly at least, because she was able to put her painful issues to good use. There's some kind of karma in that, and Neve Campbell would be the first to agree.

MICHELLE
WILLIAMS

"I HAD NO FRIENDS — AND NO ONE TO TALK TO."

Michelle, who plays Jen Lindley on *Dawson's Creek*, was introduced in the show's first episode as the new girl with a secret past. She'd come to get away from her big-city "fast crowd" and get a fresh start in quiet Capeside. Although Jen knew no one at first and it was a bumpy ride on the friendship train, she eventually got tight with Joey, Pacey, and Dawson and is now an official part of the "Dawson foursome."

When Michelle steps out of Jen's platforms, the petite actress with the perfect pout is resolutely on the fame 'n' fortune fast track. In the course of only one year, the eighteen-year-old starlet has become a sought-after magazine cover girl, Internet babe, and movie star. Michelle was second-billed (after Jamie Lee Curtis) in the thriller *Halloween: H2O* and stars in the teen comedy *Dick*, with Kirsten Dunst.

Everyone who knows Michelle mentions her sweetness, generosity, and up-for-anything personality. Behind the scenes at *Dawson's Creek* she's totally bonded with castmate Katie Holmes. The girlfriends shop, beach it, dish about guys, bake cookies together, and "just goof off." At home in Los Angeles, Michelle does quality girlfriend time with her best buds Meghan, and Amy, Michelle's housemate.

So what exactly is Michelle Williams doing in the Friendship Issues section? Talking about the bad old days, actually, when she was not only friend-challenged but worse — ostracized and picked on. Responding to a reporter's question about how she relates to her TV character, she said, "Playing Jen is like slipping into a second skin. I certainly have a lot to draw on. Everybody's got a past."

Listen in and take heart as Michelle has described the heinous, hurtful part of hers. If you saw the movie *Welcome to the Dollhouse*, you'll get the picture.

"Woof! Woof! Did you play the dog?"

Michelle knows exactly what it's like to be the new girl in town. At nine years old, she moved with her family from a tiny town in Montana to bustling, cosmopolitan San Diego, California. It wasn't easy getting used to the pace or the people. The fact that she began her acting career the following year — she started in commercials — made it that much harder to fit in at school. Often, she was pulled out of classes for auditions, and sometimes to actually film a commercial or a TV guest gig. "I can remember feeling so different from all the other kids," she has said.

But no one pushed her out of the classroom and in front of the cameras. She never wanted to do anything *but* — "It was always eat, sleep, act," she told *Teen* magazine.

At thirteen, she landed a costarring role in the movie *Lassie*, a remake of the classic family film. It made her life at school hell. As she recounted in *TV Guide*, "Every time I walked across the school yard, people would go, 'Woof! Woof! Did you play the dog?'"

The taunts got worse during her next movie, the sci-fi thriller *Species*. "I thought *Lassie* was bad," Michelle recalled, "but having worms come out of your face? Never do a sci-fi movie when you're in school."

"High school was the most miserable time of my life."

So . . . how miserable was it? Check this: Michelle could stomach only one year there — and she seems to remember every rotten day of it. "That year was so hard for me," she confessed.

Michelle went to Santa Fe Christian Upper High School. She remembers being "a social klutz, a total nerd. I always enjoyed the work," she told a reporter, "just not the social part of it. I can't pinpoint a single positive experience."

Partly, her attendance record was to blame. She was absent much because of work, and kids resented her for it. And Michelle made no bones about the fact that the bad feelings were mutual.

"I just hated the people, the atmosphere, the catty fights between the girls. The girls just didn't understand that there was life past clothes, makeup, and boys. Even the peer pressure from the guys was bad."

Her outsider status was sealed, but that year, it was more than school yard name-calling. "I had no friends and no one to talk to," she told *Teen* magazine. "If there were any good times, I don't remember them. I spent every lunch period hiding out in a stall in the bathroom. I didn't have anyone to sit with in the cafeteria."

Worse than simply being ignored, she was also picked on. Kids played cruel pranks on her.

"There was one girl who used to torture me," Michelle recounted in a magazine. "She stole my clothes out of my gym locker and hid them. Another time, she sent me a fake note from this very cute boy in my class. It read, 'Meet me by the back stairs at three P.M.' Of course, I felt like a big fool when I showed up and he wasn't there."

Worst of all, as she revealed, was being harmed physically. "Girls that age can be so petty and mean. They would take my backpack and push me down."

The combination of her horrendous experience in school and her burgeoning acting career led Michelle and her parents to a decision. And that made all the difference.

The turning point: I am outta here!

Michelle left high school after ninth grade and spent the next year being home schooled by her dad. Incredibly, she worked at warp speed and managed to cram three years of academics into one. At the end of tenth grade, following the rules of California's independent study program, she'd earned enough credits to get a high school equivalency diploma.

Soon after, she convinced her parents to allow her to become an emancipated minor. That basically means she could work as an actress without having a legal guardian around and that she had power over her earnings. Then, at sixteen, she moved out — all the way up to Los Angeles, where the acting jobs were.

"I've always had a vicious independent streak," Michelle admitted. "I love being on my own. It's been a source of agony for my parents." Of the big move, she confessed in *Jump* magazine, "[At first] my mom was hurt, but she would send me underwear and socks."

In fact, at first her parents took turns living with her, but that wasn't a practical solution, since Michelle's younger sister was still at home. Eventually, Michelle wound up living totally on her own.

Although she'd escaped the vicious swipes of schoolmates and, as a working actress, felt less like an outsider, being on her own wasn't a total pass to good times. Michelle's year of living solo certainly had its share of ups and downs. Though she declines to go into detail about a "too-long phase with these crazy friends, going to clubs and chasing what we thought Hollywood was," she does concede, "I wasn't ready for it. Don't think I'm encouraging the idea of packing up and moving out on your own. It was really hard."

Luckily, a lead role in *Dawson's Creek* was right around the corner. It took Michelle to Wilmington, North Carolina, where the show is filmed, and finally to being a total *insider*, flush with friends and a surrogate family among the cast and crew.

Back to school: "I still get the shakes . . ."

Michelle's horrible high school year left an indelible mark. She still can't shake the evil feelings, as she told a magazine. "When I visit my parents I sometimes have to go to pick up my sister, Paige, who's at the same school. When I see the girls I went to school with [who are seniors now], I still get the shakes and my stomach hurts. I revert to this ninth-grade mentality."

On the *Dawson's* set, it's much the same. "When we have all these big school hallway scenes, I still get sweaty palms," she admitted, adding, "People underestimate how tough high school can be for kids. There's pressure from all sides. You have to get good grades and look and act a certain way to fit in, and everyone thinks you need a boyfriend."

Wounded still by those bad old days, Michelle is ultrasensitive to people who don't like her character. There's an "I Hate Jen!" Internet website that makes her feel terrible. "It's disheartening to know that someone spent time and energy setting up a website to hate me," she groused to *TV Guide*.

Knowing that she's succeeding at her dream does help — a little. "The most rewarding thing is . . . the fact that everything that is happening right now is something I've always wanted." One day, maybe Michelle will even be able to distance herself and look back with less hurt. She's trying, anyway.

"Growing up, I wanted desperately to fit in. I drove myself crazy trying to be accepted. And you know what? I'm only seventeen, but I know that all that worrying was a crazy waste of time. Now, because of my friends from *Dawson's Creek*, I've begun to realize that I can make my own group. Just like our characters on the show, I feel like I'm still not the coolest, but I'm not a geek, either. I'm still figuring out who I am."

SETH GREEN

"I ABSOLUTELY DID NOT FIT IN."

Most fans know Seth Green as Oz on *Buffy the Vampire Slayer* — high school student and Willow's boyfriend by day, musician and sometime werewolf by night. The character, who started out as a part-timer on *Buffy*, got promoted to full-fledged member of the vampire-vanquishing team at the beginning of season three. Now he's in every episode.

While the young actor couldn't be more pumped about that, Oz is really just the latest in a long line of Seth Green screen creations. Remember *Austin Powers: International Man of Mystery*? Seth played Scott Evil, son of the lead character's rival. If you saw *Can't Hardly Wait*, you saw Seth as Kenny. If you watched certain episodes of *The X-Files*, *Mad About You*, or *The Drew Carey Show* . . . yep, he was in those, too. If the film *Idle Hands* is on your "wanna see it" list, you'll enjoy Seth's out-there performance as a slacker-zombie.

Truth is, Seth Green has been a working actor for most of his life. The movies and TV shows mentioned are just the most current. Seth started in the biz at the age of eight and is a veteran of commercials and dozens more roles.

The boy was a successful child actor who effortlessly made the leap into teen and young adult parts. In real life, he's sweet and funny and self-deprecating and generous. He seems to be the poster boy for all-around success. So what could his issues be? Hint: Being a child actor did not serve him well on the popularity train at school. In fact, it barred admission totally. Well, that, plus a host of other reasons.

Seth spent most of his elementary and junior high school years as an outsider. He recounts those years and what eventually happened to turn things around so that other kids who feel — and *are* — different may take heart.

"I was teased about *everything*."

"Kids tend to make fun of what they don't have or understand, and that pretty much describes everything about me when I was a kid. I was an actor, but I didn't live in Hollywood or any other place you might be among other working kids. I lived and went to public school in Philadelphia. So I was pretty much the only kid who was out of class a lot, running to New York City to go on auditions or off to Los Angeles to film a movie. I was teased about everything.

"But that wasn't the only reason kids teased and resented me. I got it for my size, my energy, and if we're honest here, my personality: I thought I was much smarter than I was. And I let everyone know it.

"I'm five feet four inches now and as you can guess, I've always been short. Shorter than most of the boys in my class and shorter even than some of the girls. That became glaringly apparent early on, because I was also a year accelerated, in with kids a year older than I. So not only was I the smallest, I was also the youngest.

"To the other kids, I also had a funny name. It was like, in my neighborhood at that time if you weren't Jimmy or Matt, if you didn't sound like a tough guy, you weren't in. To them, my name was weird. They'd call me Death instead of Seth. It didn't help that I didn't play athletics at school. Whenever it was my turn in kick-ball, everybody moved in closer.

"Even my bright red hair was cause for ridicule. So I was the short, unathletic kid with the red hair and funny name who was always leaving school for acting jobs. It was like I was asking for trouble — asking to be branded different.

"But that wasn't even all of it. I cop to it: I was obnoxious, too. My parents instilled me and my sister with a strong vocabulary, and sometimes I felt I knew more than the teachers did. You can imagine how *that* went over. I'd debate them — no teacher appreciated it. But I was self-righteous and would not be quiet. You have no idea how many times I'd hear, 'You're not being paid [to talk] now, Seth, so shut up.'

"That was at the heart of another problem. The being-a-child-actor part. If I talked about what I was doing, what movie or commercial even, I'd get ostracized. If I didn't talk about it, I'd get accused of being stuck-up — like I was too good to discuss it with them. It hurt. I felt like I should change somehow, but I had no idea how to make kids like me.

"Then, on the other hand, there was the part of my life when I was *in* the acting world. There, I was being praised for and having success because of the same traits I got put down for at school. For being talkative, articulate, a wise guy. For having red hair [which is always in demand for kids in commercials]. Even being smaller than most kids my age worked for me. As a child actor, you can play a wider range of parts for a longer period of time.

"So on the one hand, famous people like Woody Allen, for whom I starred in the movie *Radio Days*, and Johnny Carson (I was on *The Tonight Show* when I was a kid) were going on about how great I was. And on the other, everyone in school couldn't stand me."

The more you try to fit in, the more outside you are

"Mostly, I didn't dress like the other kids, either. I was wearing huge, oversized army pants, T-shirts with comic book characters on them. The other kids were all very fashionable, preppy but hip. They'd wear nice pants like khakis, sweatshirts, sneakers. Some of them wore gold chains.

"I wanted to belong. I wanted to play with them, to be cool.

"So in junior high school, I went through a phase where I tried hard to fit in, by dressing and acting like them. It was the worst thing I could have done. Because kids can smell bull a mile away. And the more you try to fit in, the more outside you're going to appear. The more cool I tried to be, the less cool I ultimately was. It took a long time for me to realize that there was nothing wrong with me. And I didn't need to feel stupid or to change in any way.

"There was one area where not being one of the guys served me well. That was with girls. I've always been really flirtatious and always had a keen respect for girls. So, like, at a school dance, when the boys stick to one side of the room and the girls huddle in the other? I would be the one guy who crosses the floor and asks someone to dance. I always knew that girls are as scared as boys, they just want the guys to make the first move. They want to have fun."

What made all the difference: Making one friend

"There were two changes in my life that really turned things around for me. They both happened around the age of fourteen. The first was outside of school. I joined a youth group and started to do things I really enjoyed. We went on retreats, we'd go to Washington, D.C., to lobby for bills we wanted passed, we'd go on trips to the Pocono Mountains, we'd run dances and sleepovers and see *The Rocky Horror Picture Show*, stuff like that. For the first time in my life I was having fun with kids who liked the same things I did. And being with them helped me find myself. Maybe more importantly, for the first time in my life I was in a place where you weren't picked on for what you looked like or for what your interests were. If you were ragged on, it was because you deserved it. Because you did something evil to someone else, hurt someone else. It was never for having red hair or a 'funny' name, or being short, or being an actor.

"The second thing that happened was in school. I finally found one kid — one friend — who understood me, who felt, dressed, and acted pretty much the same way. He wasn't a working actor, but he was into comic books and music like I was. He and I dressed the same way — when I look back, it hits me how ridiculous we must've looked. We'd wear these loud, multicolored clothes under huge black overcoats with fingerless gloves.

"We weren't trying to make a statement, and we certainly weren't trying to fit in. We were just being ourselves. And in the end, that's really what made all the difference. Because as soon as I stopped trying to fit in, everything suddenly came together — I did fit in. After a while, all the girls got into us. And at the age of fifteen, sixteen, that was more important than anything else."

" . . . It's okay to be geeky. It's okay to be an outsider."

"Okay, here's what I've learned. Like I said before, kids make fun of what they don't have, don't understand, or are afraid of. When you're young, similarities is all you have, so it's what you cling to. So if someone points and yells out, 'That guy's fat!' or 'That guy's a weirdo!' you'd rather belong to the group doing the criticizing than being the poor soul who's getting pointed at.

"But still, I've learned that it's better to be true to yourself — no matter how different other kids say you are — than to try and copy them. It's not the same as taking the offensive attitude of, 'Forget them, I'll do what I want, and I don't care about anyone else.' It's about doing stuff, wearing things, being among people who make you happy, without being disrespectful to others.

"My best advice? Recognize that what you've got is special, no matter how different you look or feel from other kids around you. Work really hard at what you love, and just know that it's okay to be geeky. It's okay to be an outsider. It's okay to be you. Take it from me."

NICK CARTER

"I LIKE TO KEEP MYSELF TO MYSELF."

The Backstreet Boys are really out there. You can't channel surf past MTV, VH1, or the Box without catching one of their hit videos. You can't switch on your car radio without singing along to their single of the moment. And you can't walk past a newsstand without seeing them on the cover of some magazine. In other words, the Backstreet Boys are hot! Wherever they go, they attract crowds of loyal fans just trying to get a glimpse of A. J., Brian, Howie, Kevin, or Nick. For the five Orlando, Florida-based boys, it's definitely been life in the spotlight, and they seem to thrive on it.

But it might surprise you to know that the "baby" Boy, Nick Carter, is something of a loner. Onstage, Nick is definitely the wild one. He dances up a storm and seems to bask in the heat of the spotlight and roar of the audience. But once he finishes the last notes of the final song and dashes offstage, eighteen-year-old Nick prefers to keep everything low-key and down low. Unless it's a business must, Nick would rather take a pass on a party and go back to his hotel room and challenge himself with a few Final Fantasy VII games on his ever-present Sony PlayStation.

"I wasn't a very social person."

It's not that the blond, six-foot-one-inch cutie is unfriendly. It's just that Nick has always marched to a different drummer. "When I was a young child, I wasn't a very social person," Nick mentioned in an interview. "I tried to stay focused. I wasn't one of the popular people in school. I was very *unpopular*. Other kids were more mature than me in a way. More grown-up. . . . Actually, maybe it was the other way around. I always liked school, but I had to leave school because I was acting and singing. They didn't understand why I left, and they were jealous in a way. Since I was around grown-ups a lot of the time, maybe I was a little more focused than the kids at school. So they didn't understand me."

Nick wasn't complaining; he just knew from early on that he had a master plan for his life and *nothing* was going to distract him. And nothing did. When Nick was only thirteen, he joined the Backstreet Boys. Not only did he find four new best friends, but Nick was finally surrounded by peers who shared his make-it-to-the-top dreams. It was a lot more comfortable for Nick in this environment, and he was able to really be himself. As for school, since the Backstreet Boys were on the road so much, Nick traveled with a full-time tutor. In May 1998, he received his high school diploma in a very unconventional "ceremony" — his tutor handed it to him in a hotel room.

Nick doesn't feel as if he really missed out on his high school days. No, he didn't go to his senior prom and didn't attend his graduation, but to Nick these were easy sacrifices to make. He was doing exactly what he wanted to do: performing for millions of people all over the world.

"Onstage I become this wild person."

His Backstreet buddies understand just who Nick is. He doesn't get grief from them if he doesn't join them for a party-hearty night. It's not that he's a dud, it's just that Nick has his own way of doing things. In a very revealing interview with *Big!* magazine, he explained: "Offstage I don't like to go to clubs. I like to keep myself to myself! The guys like to go out to parties and nightclubs, but that's not the sort of person I am. I like to play video games and spend time by myself. But onstage I become this wild person; it's not bad — in fact, it's kinda cool. But yes, I do have a kind of Jekyll and Hyde thing going on. I love to get up onstage and do all this sexy dancing, but I could never go to a club and dance like that!"

Even when Nick is back home in Tampa, he's anything but a party animal. There he likes to let his hair down and just be Nick Carter, not Nick of the Backstreet Boys. If you don't find Nick playing video games or fooling around with his two pug puppies, William and Michael, he's usually enjoying the turquoise waters of Tampa Bay or the Florida Keys. Nick's prized possession is his motorboat. "A lot of the time I go out on the boat alone. Being on my own, with just the silence of the sea, is such an escape from the constant screaming of fans on a Backstreet Boys tour. It's something I need to do — just to get away from it all. . . . The ocean does something to me that is unexplainable. . . . To me, the Florida Keys are paradise on earth."

The point is that very early on Nick knew who he was and what made him happy. He may have been different from his classmates, but that didn't make him a bad person, that didn't make him wrong. It only made him *Nick*. He understood that if he gave into peer pressure to be someone he's not, he wouldn't be happy. Sometimes it takes courage to set yourself apart from the people around you. But Nick knew that he could not live up to an image that other people might have of him — not his school friends and not his fans. He knew that there is an age-old saying that he would always follow: Be true to yourself.

Brandy
(*Moesha*/singer)

"I didn't have friends at school. [In] elementary [school] girls teased me because I was so skinny and I wasn't that pretty. They pulled my hair and tried to jump me after school. In junior high, people hated me; they thought I was trying to show off. I used to try to buy friendships with my lunch money. It was awful for me." [*US*]

LeAnn Rimes (country singer)

LeAnn has been performing all her life. Her friendship problems started in junior high school. There, kids often felt jealous — and acted out by harassing her. "I was threatened a lot," she told *USA Today*. "I did have friends, but there were these four girls who were scaring me a lot."

Melissa Joan Hart
(*Sabrina the Teenage Witch*)

"Between the ages of thirteen to eighteen, I was starring in *Clarissa Explains It All*. It was filmed in Orlando, Florida, so I was separated from family and friends. I was always working, or sitting with a tutor six hours a day. I wanted to go to school and hang out with people my age. Every time a girl came on the show [to act in an episode] I tried to be her best friend."

JENNIFER LOVE HEWITT

CHARISMA CARPENTER

MELISSA JOAN HART

Chris O'Donnell

KATE WINSLET

SCOTT VICKARYOUS

2

Baby Spice (Emma Bunton)

JERRY O'CONNELL

BODY AND SELF-IMAGE ISSUES

Drew Carey

ROSIE PEREZ

FIONA APPLE

Sarah McLachlan

Sporty Spice (Melanie Chisholm)

BRANDY

COUNTESS VAUGHN

JENNIFER ANISTON

SHANIA TWAIN

Michelle Williams

CHRISTINA RICCI

CAMERON DIAZ

LIV TYLER

JONATHAN TAYLOR THOMAS

MIA TYLER

ELISA DONOVAN

PAULA COLE

Julianna Margulies

MINNIE DRIVER

Okay, is there really anyone you know who *doesn't* have body image issues? Any friend or family member who thinks he or she is physically da bomb? Here on planet Earth, models, actors, and athletes are the people we hold up as icons of physical perfection.

If only we could look like them, we'd be happy.

Well, guess what? "Them" isn't always so happy with how they look. "Them" has — or had — the same issues you do. Even the most popular stars are not always down with what nature gave them or, often, didn't give them. And being on camera, where the whole world is watching, can make it even harder to get over those issues.

In this section, you'll hear from celebrities who sing the body issues and self-esteem blues just like you do. Some will surprise you; others may not. But it's the way they learned to deal with it, to think about it, that's made all the difference. Feel like you're too fat, too flat, too skanky, the home of the heinous honker, or crater-face central? Got body issues much? You are *so* not alone.

JENNIFER LOVE HEWITT

"I WOKE UP ONE DAY AND I THOUGHT, T-SHIRTS WILL NEVER BE THE SAME FOR ME."

Her name says it all: Love. For the past several years it seems as if Ms. Hewitt's beautiful face has adorned the covers of magazines such as *Teen*, *YM*, *Seventeen*, and *Teen People* each and every month. That's not surprising since besides her regular duties as Sarah on TV's much-watched series *Party of Five*, Love has been making back-to-back films like *House Arrest*, *I Know What You Did Last Summer*, *Can't Hardly Wait*, *I Still Know What You Did Last Summer*, and several upcoming feature flicks including *The Suburbans*. In September 1999, she'll star in her own series, a *Po5* spin-off.

It's gotten to the point where if casting agents can't get Love for a particular project, they are demanding their staffs go out and find "a Love Hewitt type." It's definitely become a flat-out Lovefest for the twenty-year-old actress.

However, if you listen to Love during one of her heart-to-heart conversations, you'll find that there was a time when Jennifer Love Hewitt would not have won any popularity or beauty contests —

at least she doesn't think so. Though singing and dancing were always second nature to Love, there was a time when she felt like an outsider.

"I never really fit in where I lived in Texas."

Turn the clock back. Check out a map of Texas. Just north of Austin is the little town of Killeen. And that's where it all began for Jennifer Love Hewitt.

Love and her older brother, Todd, who is now a chiropractor, were raised by their mom, Pat Hewitt. Love's parents had divorced when she was very young. Pat worked as a speech pathologist to support her two children. And she encouraged them to pursue the things that interested them.

From the very beginning, Love was a natural-born entertainer. Give her any excuse, and Love was putting on a show. There are those who dissed her as a little show-off, but the fact was, the little darling had *real* talent, and she wanted to express it. "I would host and direct and star in these little plays," Love wistfully recalled in a *People* magazine interview. "My friends never really wanted to do it. I always thought there was something wrong with them. . . . I never really fit in where I lived in Texas."

By the time Love was ten, she was taking dance lessons — jazz, tap, and ballet. She sang at local events. And since they were living in Texas, some of those events were livestock shows and county fairs. Even though Love's costars were sometimes cattle, pigs, and homemade baked goods, there was no hiding the fact that she was already a star.

Friends — and sometimes total strangers — urged Pat to allow her daughter to pursue a showbiz career. So when Pat was introduced to a Los Angeles manager who thought Love had great potential, the Hewitts moved to the city of dreams.

Love's dreams soon became reality. Shortly after they relocated, Love joined the cast of the TV show *Kids, Incorporated* and was signed as an L.A. Gear dancer. When Love was still just a 'tween — the time between being a little girl and a teenager — she was traveling all over the world performing at L.A. Gear exhibitions and trade shows. She even appeared with Michael Jackson once!

"I used to get Coke thrown on me."

Love didn't really have a long 'tween period, however. It seems to her that one day she was a typical little girl who played with dolls and the next she was a living, breathing Barbie doll herself. In other words, Love's breasts developed.

"I was about twelve," Love told *Movieline* magazine. "I woke up one day and I thought, T-shirts will never be the same for me. It took me a long time to get used to. For those first two or three years, I wore huge sweaters and didn't want to be a part of what was going on with me."

Being self-conscious about the natural changes her body was going through was bad enough. But Love had the added burden of not fitting in with her classmates because she was a working actress and often absent from school. "I was completely unpopular," Love confessed to the *Movieline* writer. "I had a really rough time in junior high school. My teachers didn't like me because they thought I was ruining my education, even though I was learning much more through work than they could ever have taught me in school.

The kids just thought I was some freak and tried to beat me up. I used to get Coke thrown on me."

"I think of myself as pretty average."

Well, it's been a while since Love had Coke thrown on her. Now people are throwing her compliments — and movie offers. Since those dreaded junior high days, Love has really come into her own. And she has finally become comfortable with her body. Love can't deny the fact that she does have a curvy figure. Even if she wanted to, it would be very hard to hide it on a twenty-foot-high movie screen.

Actually, Love's transformation from oversize sweaters to form-fitting outfits helped her develop a sense of humor about her image. The down-to-earth part of Love laughed when she saw the huge *Can't Hardly Wait* movie billboard that loomed over a Hollywood intersection. There, in living color and larger than life, was Love in a low-cut tank top. "Pretty revealing, huh?" she joked with a *Teen People* reporter as they drove past. Another time, when Love was at a press conference for *I Know What You Did Last Summer* and the subject of being well-endowed was brought up, Love laughed and revealed that she doesn't consider herself some kind of Hollywood bombshell. As a matter of fact, she irreverently joked that she even named her breasts Thelma and Louise!

"I don't think anybody would believe me as a very sexy person, so I'd be wasting my time," Love told her *Movieline* interviewer when he asked her if she would ever take a total-babe role. "I'm one of those people that if it came down to comparing me to Marilyn Monroe or Gidget, I'd always be Gidget."

Love has accepted what once embarrassed her. She doesn't have to hide her figure anymore. But she doesn't flaunt it, either. She understands that she is a whole package, not just a body part. She is Jennifer Love Hewitt, a total person who consists of body and brains, talent and goals, emotions and desires. In one of Love's most candid interviews, she explained her attitude about the whole sex-symbol image. "We all have days when we look at ourselves and go, 'I look pretty darned good today,' but I think of myself as pretty average," she told *Teen* magazine. "I'm flattered by fan letters that say they think I'm gorgeous, or when a magazine says, 'We're putting together our hundred sexiest women issue and you're in it,' and I think, 'You should really rethink that!' You can't be an actress and not be concerned about how you look, but I'm glad I don't focus on it that much. You kinda have to realize that the Creator who put you on this earth wanted you to be who you are and look how you look. If everybody looked the same — perfect, beautiful, clear skin — it would be boring. You can play around, try new, exciting things — makeup, a new hairstyle — but you can't really change how you look — it makes you who you are."

P.S.: Remember Love's junior high tormentors? Love certainly did when she ran into two of them not long ago. It was at a 7-Eleven near Love's house. "It was really cool," Love giggled during her *Movieline* interview as she recalled the run-in. "I went in to get a Slurpee and they were standing there. I got that old fear back, like, 'Oh, my God.' Then they came up to me and they said, 'We just love *Party of Five*. Would you mind signing something?' And I said, 'You know what? I'm sorry, I can't. I have to go. Really nice to see you. Bye-bye.' I wanted to say something really mean, but why go to their level?"

KATE WINSLET

"THEY CALLED ME THE BABY WHALE."

Kate Winslet sped to fame aboard the most famous movie of our time, *Titanic*. As society girl Rose DeWitt Bukater, she dumps her wealthy, abusive fiancé for free-spirited struggling artist Jack Dawson. He turns out to be her soulmate. Alas, their love is tragically doomed.

How great was Kate in the role? She nabbed an Academy Award nomination for her moving portrayal. And that wasn't even the first time she'd been touched by an Oscar. Kate made the 1996 list for her supporting role in *Sense and Sensibility*. Two nominations is pretty cool. Getting them both before the age of twenty-three is pretty amazing.

But hello, it's neither Kate's awesome talent nor her brilliant beauty that made her the envy of millions of girls. It's that Jack was played by Leonardo DiCaprio. Sharing love scenes with Leo, spending seven months sequestered with him and coming away with his deep, abiding friendship? The line for the girls who'd have traded places with her in a heartbeat starts here.

What most fans *wouldn't* envy, however, is what came along with the friendship, fortune, and fame brought about by *Titanic.* Her own personal iceberg, you might say: the berating of Kate. The suddenly famous actress has been subjected to harsh and mean-spirited criticism, not only by a tsk-tsking, finger-wagging press, but also famously by her own director. The subject? Her weight.

While she was svelte as *Titanic's* Rose, Kate is the first to admit she's not naturally predisposed toward being slim. And when her "natural generous proportions" (her term) returned after the movie, she got dissed — loudly, publicly, constantly. To most actresses, the barbs, coupled with unflattering photos, would have been totally humiliating. But British-born Kate is unlike most body-conscious Hollywood starlets. In fact, the obsession with her weight is really an issue for *others*: As you'll see, *she's* quite at home in her skin. Hers is a refreshing attitude: Check it.

"I was very fat as a baby."

Although the issue of Kate's weight has been brought up time and again, not once has she felt the need to apologize for it. As if it were the most natural thing in the world, she described to a London newspaper, "I was a very fat baby, and as a child, I was almost obese . . . they called me the baby whale."

She elaborated in *Rolling Stone*: "I was chubby as a child; my old nickname was 'Blubber.' It was a family thing. My uncle is a chef. My mother is a fantastic cook. We're all big eaters. It was kind of unavoidable."

It never really bothered her. It certainly didn't hamper her. Kate is from a family of actors, going back to her grandparents and including her siblings. She got her professional start at the age of twelve, when she was cast in a TV commercial. At fifteen, she landed her first TV series.

At sixteen, she stood five feet six inches tall and weighed 185 pounds. It was during the filming of a British TV movie that her weight first became a concern to her. Kate happened to be playing the daughter of a very heavyset woman. One day the director said he noticed an "extraordinary resemblance" between the mother-and-daughter actresses.

Kate freaked. "I looked at this woman who weighed nearly three hundred pounds and thought, This has got to change. I wouldn't work if I stayed this way." She joined Weight Watchers. One year later, she'd slimmed down considerably.

That was the beginning of a brief obsession with her weight. The worst time, she mentioned in a newspaper interview, was a bout with anorexia at the age of eighteen.

Afterward, she said in *Movieline*, "By nineteen, I'd gone from pillar to post about my body and spent at least ninety-five percent of my headspace every day thinking about what I bloody looked like," adding in another interview, "I went through all the paranoias, my bum's massive, my breasts are saggy, I've got a spotty back."

What got her through the self-deprecation were some sincere words of wisdom and a book, both given by a valued friend. "When I was making *Sense and Sensibility*, Emma Thompson noticed that I'd skip lunch and not eat properly. She said, 'If you dare try and lose weight for this job, I will be furious with you.' She went out and bought me [the book] *The Beauty Myth*, and since then, I've been much more relaxed about that side of it."

Lucky for her that she was over her own body image issues before she set sail on the *Titanic*. Because the attention that came her way was as massive and unavoidable as that iceberg. Much of it was massively unkind.

"Kate Weighs-a-Lot"

It was reported in *Rolling Stone* that during the strenuous *Titanic* shoot, when nerves were frayed and sleep deprivation ruled, James Cameron once called his lead actress Kate Weighs-a-Lot. No one's denied it; everyone jokes about it. "I changed it to Kate Whines-a-Lot," the director allegedly commented later.

At the Golden Globe Awards, at which *Titanic* won Best Picture, Kate was photographed wearing a body-clinging black lace dress. The picture was published more often than it might have been, because Kate's dress made it obvious that her natural generous proportions had returned. No way could she fit into Rose's corseted costumes. That was cause for a great deal of public snickering.

In an article (humorously?) titled "Girth of a Nation," about a new trend, how it might be "hip to be hippy," *Entertainment Weekly* ran Kate's photo alongside those of hefty actresses Kathy Kinney (Mimi on *The Drew Carey Show*), Camryn Manheim (*The Practice*), and chunky cartoon character Cartman from *South Park*.

In spite of an outcry from Kate's fans, the dissing hardly ended there. In what was perhaps the nastiest comment of all, it was reported that the jewelers who created a $3.5 million replica of *Titanic*'s Heart of the Ocean sapphire-and-diamond necklace refused to allow Kate to wear it at the Academy Awards. "She's rather fat and disheveled," was the quote of one exec. (Of course, they also refused to allow Gloria Stuart to wear it, sniffing, "She's not really our ideal candidate.") Instead, pencil-thin Celine Dion wore it as she warbled "My Heart Will Go On."

There seems to be no end in sight to the attention — and the criticism. Long after the *Titanic* spotlight should have faded, the press is still at it. In the summer of 1998, a newspaper erroneously reported that Kate was asked to play Arnold Schwarzenegger's wife in his new movie — *if* she agreed to drop ten pounds. Another tattled that she was furiously trying to lose weight for a revealing scene with Harvey Keitel in the movie *Holy Smoke*.

Yet another account had her up for the lead in the movie adaptation of the book *Bridget Jones's Diary* — mainly because the title character is chubby.

"Life is short, and it's here to be lived."

That Kate allowed none of the snickering to bother her isn't a bow to her acting ability. It really *doesn't* bother her. Partly, it's *The Beauty Myth* book and the attitude shared with her by Emma Thompson. Kate has taken that to heart.

Poignantly, it's also because she knows what's important in life — and what's not. Recently Kate suffered through the loss of her first love, a man who was as close to her as Jack was to Rose. His name was Stephen Tredre, and he died of bone cancer at a very young age. "When someone close to you dies, it throws a hell of a lot into perspective," Kate has sagely said.

And partly, it's also the understanding that being a real actress isn't about glamour — and glamour isn't about being thin. As Kate expressed in *Movieline*, "Acting is about being real, being honest. Ultimately, the audience doesn't love you or want to be with you because of what your face looks like or the size of your backside. They've got to love you because of the honesty within your soul."

That honesty allows Kate to be Kate: a young woman who is exuberant, passionate, and who refuses to stress about an extra inch, an extra pound. It allows her to express her feelings to fans as she did in several magazines.

"Some people are naturally very slim. I'm naturally curvy. I've been to hell and back with my weight, and I'm finally happy the way I am. I feel my responsibility is to say to young women who are in turmoil about their weight: Life is short, and it's here to be lived."

CHRISTINA RICCI

"FOR YEARS I HATED MYSELF. I COVERED THE MIRRORS IN MY HOUSE."

Born in Santa Monica, California, Christina Ricci is the youngest of four children. Her mother, Sarah, was a former Ford model, and her father, Ralph, a lawyer-turned-therapist. They divorced when Christina was just entering her teens.

Early on it was obvious that Christina liked to entertain. "She lives for making her brothers and sister laugh," Sarah Ricci once told *People* magazine about Christina. When the Riccis moved three thousand miles east to Montclair, New Jersey, seven-year-old Christina brought the acting bug with her from California. While she was still in grade school, Christina was in a school pageant and was noticed by a local movie critic. He commented to the Riccis that Christina had real talent and said that they might consider getting her into acting. Within a year, she got work in commercials and landed her first feature film role, costarring with Cher in *Mermaids*.

That was just the beginning. Today, the eighteen-year-old actress's résumé includes films such as *The Addams Family*, *Addams Family Values*, *Now and Then*, *Casper*, *Gold Diggers: The Secret of*

Bear Mountain, *The Ice Storm*, and *The Opposite of Sex*, as well as many others.

With all those films to her credit, it might surprise you to know that Christina does not see herself as a movie star. As a matter of fact, for years she has battled with her self-image. Christina has always said exactly what was on her mind — even if it was sometimes blunt or biting. But she never excused herself from the barbs. During an interview with *Premiere* magazine, the five-foot-two-inch fifteen-year-old Christina was supercritical of herself as the makeup artist and hairstylist readied her for the accompanying photo session. "I've never had a growth spurt. I may be short for the rest of my life. . . . And I have the biggest forehead. I have this *huge* forehead, and I guess when I was little, I kept hitting my head in the same spot, so I have these two, like, permanently thickened places, these two *knobs!*"

"I was really fat. . . . I was ugly."

And then there's Christina's concern over her weight — a worry that eventually led her to a bout with anorexia. As she went from child actress to teen roles, she was getting mixed signals from the showbiz types who were all around her.

When Christina first began to develop, she was still going on auditions for kids' roles. In another interview with *Premiere*, Christina revealed how thoughtless some people were. "For years when I went on auditions, people would tell me, 'Hide your chest. Make sure you don't wear anything tight,'" she said. "They would put this binding stuff on me so I would be flat chested. It was annoying as hell, and it hurt at the end of the day."

One of the producers of *Gold Diggers: The Secret of Bear Mountain* even had the nerve to say to Christina, "'You look a little thick on top. What do you think we can do about your [breasts]?' He wasn't very tactful. Not used to working with young girls."

Today Christina calls those years her "teenage awkward phase." Actually, she's a lot more biting. To *Movieline*, she said, "I got ugly. Throughout my childhood, my favorite [rejection] was: 'She looks too healthy.' They wanted that really gaunt, runaway girl kind of look. I was, like, 'Mom, I thought you could never be too healthy.' She said, 'Ignore them.'"

Needless to say, those mixed messages took their toll on Christina. "I love what I do, and I hate to be one of those people who harps on how detrimental it is to development," she explained to *Premiere*. "But I do think it's bad that I felt embarrassed about my body. I had a huge backlash after *Now and Then*. I didn't want to look like a woman. I put on so much weight it was ridiculous. I mean, in *The Ice Storm* I was huge. For a long time I didn't get any work. People were not nice to me at all. They'd come up to me and say, 'Gosh, you got fat!'"

In another conversation, this time with *Interview* magazine, Christina recalled, "I was really fat for a year. I was ugly. People would come up to me in the street and say, 'Weren't you Wednesday in *The Addams Family*? God, you've gotten so fat.' I felt I was a separate person from the person they were talking about, and I'd want to take them aside and scold them: 'You can't talk to me like that.' Being overweight made it so hard for me to get films. I didn't work for a year because of it, and it was devastating."

"At first you think it's cool . . . and after a while you *cannot stop.*"

Christina's reaction was extreme but almost understandable. She was hurt and didn't know how to express herself. She was in a vicious circle. She was going through a normal body development phase, but she was in a business that demanded a Kate Moss look. "For years I hated myself," Christina admitted in her talk with *Movieline.* "I covered the mirrors in my house. I literally couldn't have a mirror in my room. I still can't sit in a restaurant or someplace where I can catch my reflection. I got so paranoid. . . . Now, though, I'm getting more comfortable. I never thought I'd be so comfortable with myself, my body. I mean, you know that I was anorexic for a year, right?"

Actually, it was more like two years. Her yo-yo weight loss and gain period began when she was around fourteen. Usually anorexia sort of sneaks up on teens. They start a diet to lose a little weight, and because of a false body image, they keep going down to dangerous levels. Christina's anorexia was a bit different. She consciously chose it. "I saw this TV movie with that girl from *Growing Pains*, Tracey Gold," she told *Time Out New York* magazine. "And I was like, 'This is so melodramatic.' But the drama of it kind of pulled me in, so I decided to do that. I thought it would be a great way to get attention. 'I'm gonna get really sick so everyone will have to come visit me in the hospital!' But then it just gets out of control. It's like being a drug addict — at first you think it's cool and romantic, and after a while you *cannot stop.*"

When Christina finally realized she had to get control of this eating disorder, she found out it wasn't so easy. With help, she tried to establish normal eating patterns again. But when she began eating properly, she not only regained the weight she had lost but gained more. "My metabolism was so slow that I put on tons of weight," she told *Interview*. "So it all started again. It was a huge ordeal."

Christina eventually learned that her problem wasn't *just* the actual weight. It was also her perception of herself and trying to become what she thought others wanted her to be. The young actress began taking her recovery one step at a time. This time she didn't go to extremes. "Just in the past three months, I've lost twenty pounds," Christina told an *Interview* reporter during the promotion period for *The Ice Storm*. "I don't feel I'm beautiful now, but I feel I'm much more attractive than I was, and life's so much easier."

However, as she continued chatting with the reporter, Christina revealed that she still had setbacks — not in starving herself, but about her self-image. "I like the fact that I look like a woman now, and at the same time, I'll go to a photo shoot and apologize to the stylist because I don't look like a model!"

Today, Christina is in an even better place than her post–*Ice Storm* days. She's made six back-to-back films and has gotten killer reviews for them. She has graduated from high school and is even considering taking a break from acting for a while to study at Columbia University's Creative Writing Department. But most important, Christina has dealt with the diet demons and the push-and-pull demands of her profession. And she has come out of it with a very *positive* attitude about herself. In a recent interview in *Premiere*, she happily admitted, "I want to look like a teen woman. I don't want to look like someone else. This is who I am. This is what I look like."

CHARISMA CARPENTER

"I WAS SELF-CONSCIOUS ABOUT MY BUBBLE BUTT."

When Charisma Carpenter first went to audition for *Buffy the Vampire Slayer*, she hoped to snare the lead role of the Slayer herself. But when casting directors saw her tape, they decided she'd make a way more convincing Cordelia Chase.

At the time, Cordelia was Sunnydale High's reigning snob queen. Everything about her was da bomb: her hair, her clothes, her makeup, friends, boyfriends . . . and, of course, there was that rockin' bod. Tall, curvy, and confident, she had it all. She looked like a girl other high school girls would envy.

Cordelia's body image issues? As if. Her attitude was "If you've got it, flaunt it." To that end, Cordelia's clothes — in the first season, anyway — were always just a little bit tighter, a little bit shorter than everyone else's.

On-screen, Charisma the actress carried herself with Cordelia's trademark haughtiness. Offscreen, however, she was far from comfortable with it. In real life, Charisma hasn't been exempt from body image issues — they've cropped up time and again, but never so powerfully as during that first season of *Buffy*. That's when she had to deal with her body issue insecurities. How she did just that might inspire you to think differently about your own.

"Maybe I didn't look so good . . ."

Charisma — yes, it is her real name; her mom got it from a perfume bottle, and it's pronounced Ca-*riz*-ma — is a native of Las Vegas, Nevada. Her memories of her childhood self-image are positive. "When I was a kid," Charisma has said, "I thought I looked great. My mom was, like, Miss Naples in her day. And she'd always put me in pageants and stuff like that. Pageants didn't make me preoccupied with how I looked. My mom's attitude was healthy, so I didn't feel pressured to look a certain way, and I actually gained a lot of self-confidence from it. It was a positive experience for me."

As Charisma grew, she eventually gave up beauty pageants to concentrate on a new passion, ballet lessons. She loved her daily rehearsals, and along with her cousins, gave many local performances. As a bonus, staying fit for ballet reinforced her positive sense of self and body image.

When Charisma was thirteen, her life changed, starting with her family's move to a small Mexican town south of Rosarito. She didn't attend a neighborhood school but commuted daily to not one but *two* different schools. Both were in the USA, in just-over-the-border Chula Vista, outside San Diego, California. She explained, "I went to one school for academics, then I'd take a bus to a magnet school that specialized in the arts — music, dance, theater."

Charisma claims she didn't fit in at either school, but it was definitely worse at the academically oriented one. "It was very social statusy, people were judged by the clothes they wore and the kind of car their families had. It wasn't that I didn't have cute clothes, but these weren't things I cared about," she told a reporter.

Still, it wasn't her sense of self that suffered. That didn't happen until later. She confessed, "I had a pretty hard time in high school. I was picked on. My hair was too permed."

The moment that forced a change in the way she felt about her body happened a little later in high school. "I had my wisdom teeth pulled and I lost a lot of weight, and you started to see my cheekbones, and I started to mature at the same time. People would say [admiringly], 'Wow, you lost a lot of weight.' And that's when it dawned on me, maybe I didn't look so good before."

Charisma didn't exactly become obsessed with her looks, but the moment did give her pause. The seeds of self-doubt that had been planted suddenly took root. They erupted at the worst possible time: just as she won the part of Cordelia.

Immediately, the wardrobe designers created outfits for her that were tighter and shorter than those worn by Sarah Michelle Gellar and Alyson Hannigan. How much tighter and shorter? Enough so that she was massively uncomfortable, and enough so that reporters noticed. They questioned her about a particular micromini she wore in a group publicity shot. "I would never wear dresses that short — oh, God, no — no way," she gasped in response.

"These pants were the tightest ever. I was miserable."

Because Charisma was new to showbiz, she didn't feel comfortable complaining to the wardrobe department. Not that time, anyway. But during the filming of an episode called "The Puppet Show," she finally spoke up. Here's why.

"They had me in these pants. They were the tightest ever. I was miserable." She explained, "Everybody has their thing — one aspect of their body that they don't really care for. Mine's my bubble butt. These pants accentuated my very, very bubbly butt.

"It wasn't the first time I'd been asked to wear things I don't like or feel comfortable wearing, but I never felt I could just go and say to the wardrobe person, 'No, I'm not wearing this.' I had to be more diplomatic. So I told her that I wanted to wear something that would hide it, like you would in high school."

"... As long as we're strong and healthy, we should ... be proud of who we are ..."

The discussion that followed changed exactly *nothing* about Cordelia's clothes — and totally *everything* about Charisma's attitude. It was a real eye-opener.

Charisma explained, "The wardrobe person is Scandinavian, and she couldn't understand my reluctance to wear something that accentuates a body part I didn't feel good about. In [American] society, the woman's body seems to be something that we hide. We don't appreciate all the different shapes and sizes that there are. So we're more self-conscious. We're all subject to that.

"She explained that females come in all shapes and sizes, and we shouldn't feel self-conscious about our bodies. 'Be who you are and be proud,' this woman said, 'because as long as we're strong and healthy, we should just be proud of who we are.'

"This is getting very philosophical for a discussion about tight pants or miniskirts, but if in some way I might be able to set some sort of example for girls who watch the show, it would be worthwhile. I don't necessarily encourage high school girls to wear skirts that are just under their butt cheeks, but just to be a little less self-conscious. I spent a lot of time trying to feel comfortable with my own self. And in some way I want to get that across. We have to be proud of who we are and what we look like. And if my butt's hanging out and my legs don't look thin enough, oh, well! I'm strong and I'm healthy. That's what's important."

The upshot? She stopped worrying about what Cordelia was wearing and began to concentrate on just staying healthy, eating food that's nutritionally sound, and exercising regularly. Not to look better, but to be healthier, to feel better. It's a message Charisma hopes to convey to anyone out there with body image issues.

ELISA DONOVAN

"I AM RECOVERING FROM ANOREXIA NERVOSA. . . . I STILL STRUGGLE WITH IT."

As Amber on the TV series *Clueless*, Elisa Donovan is always getting into sticky situations that require making heavy decisions, such as matching her shoes with her bag or choosing to which designer of the minute to give her fashion-victim allegiance. Along with actresses Rachel Blanchard, who plays Cher, and Stacey Dash, who is Dionne in the series, Elisa has spent three seasons cruising the halls of Beverly Hills High in search of "Baldwins" (good-looking guys) and avoiding "Barnies" (read geeks).

Actually, even before she was cast in the UPN TV series, Elisa, who is now twenty-six, had already perfected her snobby attitude in the 1995 hit feature film *Clueless*, which spun off the TV series.

A native of Long Island, New York, Elisa had been acting since she was seven. She was also very athletic and took gymnastics and dance classes. As a student at Northport High School, she really caught the acting bug and appeared in school productions. The five-foot-six-inch, one-hundred-twenty-pound Elisa was very popular and active during her high school years.

When she was nineteen, Elisa moved to Manhattan to study acting at the Michael Chekhov Studio. She supported herself as a bartender and appeared in Off-Broadway productions. Next came a recurring role on the now-canceled soap opera *Loving*. In 1994 she turned down a regular role on the soap and headed west. Almost immediately upon her arrival in Los Angeles, Elisa landed a guest spot as Joey Lawrence's girlfriend on *Blossom*. After appearing on a few episodes of *Blossom*, Elisa costarred in the TV movie *Encino Woman* and won the role of Ginger on *Beverly Hills, 90210*.

Shortly after, she was cast in *Clueless*. Elisa loved the off-the-wall, superficial swirl of the *Clueless* do-or-die trendsetters and residents of the Beverly Hills hip zip.

Clueless land was definitely different from Elisa's own personal experience. Comparing her reel life with her real life in an interview with *People* magazine, Elisa explained, "I love that Amber says what's on her mind. I'm much more careful about what I say and wanting to please everyone. I love clothing and how different outfits make you feel, but I'm not obsessed with it. I'm not willing to go to the extent that Amber would to look good."

However, there was a time when Elisa was willing to go a lot further than Amber to look good, to be perfect. And it wasn't funny. From 1993 to 1995 Elisa's life was totally controlled by the psychological eating disorder anorexia nervosa. Because today many preteen and teenage girls are battling this dangerous dieting syndrome (sometimes, literally, to death), Elisa wants to tell her story, which she hopes will help them see that the syndrome can be conquered.

No going back

"It started in 1992, into 1993. Body image and feelings of being fat and trying to control my weight is something I struggled with from the time I was thirteen. I was a gymnast and a dancer. I rode horses competitively. I was never overweight. But still, I would look at myself in the mirror, and I would seem heavy. Then I would look at specific body parts, and they would seem *enormous*. Completely unacceptable.

"When I was growing up, I didn't talk about it. I knew that people felt I was thin or fit, and I didn't want to seem like one of those people who wanted other people to say I was thin. I remember thinking about it when I was a junior in high school. I was hanging out with a friend of mine who was bulimic. She was throwing up to control her weight. I didn't understand it. I didn't know why you would do that. But I had already been trying to control my weight and my body prior to that. But I didn't think I had a problem. It wasn't until I got out of high school, lived in New York, and moved to Los Angeles, that I realized I was in trouble.

"In a lot of cases anorexia starts when a child moves away from their safe environment. I identify it with leaving a place I knew. Because I moved out of my parents' home and moved to New York City right after I graduated high school. The problem started to progress when I was living in New York that first year, because of the pressures I had put on myself to succeed as an actress. The pressure was really great. It definitely snowballed at that point. Once I realized how to starve — to deny myself food — there was no going back."

Food control means power

"It was gradual. At first I just ate no fats. Then I was constantly trying to eat less. I would just eat cereal and toast for breakfast in the morning and then not eat again until night. I would slowly shove off portions of food. There was a day I remember sitting at a meal with a couple of people and I was able to push the food away from me. I didn't notice it at the moment, but the conversation I was having with these people was making me uncomfortable. Not so uncomfortable that I felt threatened, but uncomfortable enough so I couldn't say what I wanted to say. I couldn't express myself. I remember pushing the food away and feeling really powerful. In a sense, that was my voice. I see now how often I would do that — use that power over food as my strength. That made me better than everyone else.

"By the spring of 1994, I literally started dropping pounds very quickly, because I was just eating a little yogurt in the morning and some fruit during the day. When I would look at myself, I would think, *I like that I am losing weight*. I liked that it was going in that direction. But I would still see what needed to be lost. The more I lost, the happier I thought I would be. But that didn't happen. I would find more little things about me. I was never thin enough."

But Elisa was down to ninety pounds, thirty pounds less than she was in high school. She was living in Los Angeles, sharing an apartment with a roommate — Jennifer Maisel — and adding role after role to her acting résumé. From Elisa's perspective, everything was going as planned. She just had to lose a little more weight and everything would be *perfect*.

"Some friends would tell me I was too thin, that I was losing too much weight. But I didn't see any of that. I thought I still needed to lose a little bit more.

"I passed out several times in restaurants when I was with friends of mine. My hair was thinning. I had a lot of hair. I had long hair. But it was thinning out and falling out. Clumps of hair would fall out when I was in the shower. My nails were broken, and especially the skin on my hands was cracked. It was aging almost. It was so strange, because I would say to my roommate, 'I wonder what's wrong with my skin? My fingers — the skin is cracking and really dry.'

"She knew what was going on and she said, 'You have to eat something. You don't have any nutrients in your body.' And I said, 'No, no, that's not it. I think there is something wrong with my skin.'

"At this time I was auditioning and working. And that's the scary thing to me. I thought I wouldn't get a job if I wasn't starving. I was confusing things. I couldn't think straight. I sort of became numb. My whole life had become really small. All it revolved around was *not* eating. Literally.

"If I wasn't working, I would get up, work out, drink coffee, and then I would read and think about how much time I could wait before I could eat my grapes. Or I would go to the market and be there for an hour, going up and down the aisles, trying to find food that had no calories. I would always end up with a bag of grapes.

"All those minor brushes, those times I passed out, those little things, I dismissed as something else. I never thought someday I would have to eat something or die. I don't know what I was thinking."

"I was really scared."

In January 1995, Elisa's world turned upside down. She had just started working on the film *Clueless*. Careerwise, things had never been better for Elisa. But one night when she was in her apartment, her heart started pounding. She couldn't breathe and felt as if her heart were going to explode. Elisa didn't realize that she had denied her body of nutrients to such an extent that she was dehydrated and close to death. Jennifer Maisel, her roommate, rushed her to Midway Hospital Medical Center in Los Angeles, and Elisa was admitted immediately. The doctors filled her body with nutrients and liquids, and Elisa responded.

"At that point I was really scared. The next morning, I got out of the hospital. My roommate took me home, and I called a nutritionist. I was given the number of a therapist also. I called both of them and started to meet with them.

"But the reason I wanted to recover was that I was afraid I would lose my job. It didn't have *anything* to do with wanting to be healthy. I wanted to make everyone else feel better so I wouldn't ruin my job situation.

"But as I started working with the nutritionist and therapist, I realized how small my life had become. I didn't go out with people. I couldn't go out to meet someone for dinner or lunch, because I couldn't eat anything. I was in a constant state of being unhappy with myself, so I didn't answer my phone.

"I was very smiley at work, but there were people who knew things were wrong. Some of them said things. Some didn't because they didn't think it was their place."

"It's a very slow recovery process."

Elisa continued to work with her nutritionist and therapist. And she began to gain weight. But it wasn't easy. There were times Elisa slipped back into her old dieting ways — especially when she feared she was gaining *too* much weight. Eventually Elisa realized that fighting her anorexia was going to be a lifetime project.

"I definitely fear falling back into it. It's a very slow recovery process. I think I'm lucky that I started to recover when I did. Often, the longer the anorexia goes on, the more difficult it is to recover. You see, you're so set in your mind; you've created these rules, and it's impossible to break them down.

"It's only been in the last year that I've really felt, okay, this is the body I'm in, and I can't manipulate it anymore. I still think about what I eat — all the time. I still check in with my nutritionist to make sure I'm eating enough and that I'm not tricking myself. And I see a therapy group of anorexics and bulimics. It has really helped me a lot. I'm also working with a trainer. But it's really, really difficult. Anorexia is not something that just goes away. I hope someday that it will just be a fleeting thought in my head and will pass away. I'm on my way there, but it's definitely still present in my life."

Watch out for the warning signs

Because *Clueless* is so popular with teens, many of Elisa's fans are at the age where anorexia first strikes. She hopes her own struggle with this disorder will ring a bell with them before it's too late. And she hopes that her recovery will show those who are already caught up in the vicious cycle of anorexia that it can be conquered. The first step is to recognize the warning flags of anorexia in yourself or in a friend. Elisa says there are some telltale signs to watch out for.

"For yourself, if your weight becomes something that decides whether or not you're a good person or successful, that's a serious warning sign. There is no connection between the shape of your body and whether you can succeed or whether you are a smart or good person. Also, if you start having battles in your head about food, that's another sign. It could be a debate over whether you should or should not eat something, or you start feeling certain foods shouldn't touch each other on your plate, or you think that any kind of food is 'bad.'

"For parents or friends, if someone you care about starts to lose a lot of weight quickly, that's an obvious sign. But more subtly, if you hear someone giving excuses not to eat like 'I've already eaten' or 'I'll eat later,' be alert. Another sign is if someone starts being very ritualistic with their food at home — like they start to cut up things in very small pieces and not eat very much.

"But don't overreact. You don't want to put chains on your kid and make them crazy. It's just being aware. Sometimes parents try to help by saying things like 'If you don't eat, you're going to die' or 'You have to be a healthy person to survive.' I knew that, and my parents constantly telling me that wasn't going to make me eat. You have to get underneath those things, get to the reason you starve yourself. Forcing someone to eat doesn't help, because ultimately anorexia is *not* about food. It's about a coping mechanism and control, striving for perfection — all things that have nothing to do with food."

COUNTESS VAUGHN

"I'M NOT TWIGGY."

For the past several years, fans of TV's *Moesha* have come to know and appreciate the character of Kim Parker. She's Mo's out-there best friend, the one who wears notice-me neon, the loudest, most creative outfits in the school. And even though Kim can't help but be aware that slim girls are considered the most attractive, *this* girl is cool with her self-image — most of the time, anyway. For that reason, Kim is one of TV's most important role models.

The actress who plays her, Countess Vaughn, twenty, is aware of her unique status. She notes, "I'm not Twiggy, and I'm not three hundred pounds. I'm in between, and you don't see a lot of that on TV. My fans appreciate my image."

Just like Kim, in real life Countess wears her self-respecting 'tude on her sleeve as well. Despite a childhood during which she was often taunted for how she looked, despite even *now* being publicly dissed by one of her costars, despite all the negativity, Countess know she's okay just they way she is. "I love myself for who I am," she asserts. Here's her story.

"Everything changed when I hit puberty. . . . I hated it."

"It's funny, all this body image stuff. As a kid, I was very skinny, but that didn't make me feel attractive. I had teeth missing, I was bony. I was just this little geeky girl. But it didn't really bother me. Back then, I got teased mainly for my name. It *is* my real name, and I had nothing to do with it, but they called me Countless, Accountable, stuff like that.

"But beyond that, I was really the cool kid, the kid other kids wanted to hang out with. I'd climb the monkey bars, I'd wrestle with the boys, I was always a tomboy, always very active.

"Everything changed when I hit puberty. I got boobies when I was nine, and that kind of messed everything up. I was in fourth grade, and I had to wear a bra. I hated it. I resented that I couldn't play like I was a tomboy anymore, I couldn't wrestle anyone. 'Cause someone always managed to pull the bra strap — mostly guys snapping it and going, 'What's that?'

"None of the other girls wore bras yet, and they were envious. They'd say things like, 'You're a woman now. You think you're so much with those.' I'd watch as all the girls talked about making their own breasts look bigger. That annoys me to this day. Back then, all I wanted to be able to do was wear a little T-shirt with no bra. I couldn't do that then. It's *never* gonna happen now."

"You're cute, but you look like you swallowed a baseball."

"My worst time was junior high school, when I began having problems with my thyroid. The Adam's apple in my throat got really big, and my eyes looked like they were popping out. I'd try to wear makeup to compensate and turtlenecks every day.

"But this was when I started dating, and that made it really hard. One boy actually did say to me, 'You're cute, but you look like you swallowed a baseball.' Eventually, I began getting radiation treatments and everything went back to normal size, but I have to take medication for the rest of my life.

"My weight began to fluctuate around that time, too. Although I've never stayed heavy for more than three months, I was no longer skinny. That's when the teasing started. I got called Fat Girl, Big Breasts, Big Butt, and worse. It was really hurtful."

I don't care what you weigh — you're beautiful and you're loved

"During those years, I did not have many girlfriends. But I was lucky that I always had guy friends, and I had a supportive family around me all the time. That's what helped me get through the rough patches of junior high and high school. I was always close to my girl cousin and to my mom. When you have a supportive family around you, you always have someone to cry on.

"I know it's not healthy to be overweight, but it's worse to be teased for being overweight. No matter what, kids need to know they're loved, and I did. My mother would say to me, 'Always think positive and hang around positive people. I don't care if you weigh ninety pounds or two hundred pounds, you're beautiful and you're loved.'

"That helped a lot, but so did growing up. Not that the teasing stopped. At every new level, there's a new devil — there's always some drama. People will forever talk. But I can't worry about what anyone else says. I also believe that the insults I took for all those years made me strong. People are so busy putting others down, they don't focus on their own lives and fulfill their own potential. I mean, where are those girls now? What are they making of their lives?

"Now, I'm not saying I'm not cute, but I'm never going to be Twiggy. And I believe there's a reason that I'm not. There's a reason for everything and everyone. I mean, it might be nice to have a slim body, but you know what? We don't get it *all*. No one gets it all. And I've been given a lot. God has given me the gift of being able to entertain people. I get paid to do what I love — making people laugh — and that makes me feel so good inside.

"I'm happy with myself and it shows. I've got family, friends, I'm doing movies [her latest is *G's Trippin'*, a comedy with *Clueless*'s Donald Adeosun Faison] and *Moesha*, and I'm in a great relationship right now.

"I get lots of mail from girls who see Kim as a role model. I like that. Here's what I write back: 'Instead of worrying about what you don't have, be proud of what you do have. Take care of yourself, be healthy, be positive. It'll show — it'll come through. If you're truly happy with yourself, it will show. And you'll be as beautiful on the outside as you already are on the inside.'"

JONATHAN TAYLOR THOMAS

"I REALIZE THAT I'M SMALLER THAN OTHER KIDS MY AGE."

When Jonathan Taylor Thomas was just a toddler, his mother, Claudine, recognized something special about him. It wasn't *just* because Jonathan was her son; there was a special spark in him. "Even when he was eighteen months old," Claudine told *People*, "he seemed older than his age, and he was really outgoing."

When the family moved from Bethlehem, Pennsylvania, to Sacramento, California, Jonathan was four and a half years old and his brother, Joel, was eight. It wasn't long after the move that Jonathan put to use his "something special." He started modeling, and when he was eight he landed a major TV commercial for Burger King.

The camera loved Jonathan, and viewers couldn't keep their eyes off the blond-haired, blue-eyed cutie when he came on-screen. And when this little guy spoke — well, his husky, almost-man-sized voice was an unexpected addition to his appeal. "I thought the whole idea of being on TV, being recognized, and having a good time was interesting," the now seventeen-year-old actor told *People* around the time he was the voice of the young Simba in Disney's *The Lion King*.

In 1991, when Jonathan was nine years old, his parents split up. His dad, Stephen, stayed in northern California, and Claudine moved Jonathan and Joel down to L.A. And that was a major step for Jonathan's career. The TV sitcom *Home Improvement* was his big break. Millions of viewers all over America, and eventually the rest of the world, fell in love with the Taylor family headed by actor Tim Allen. As Randy, the middle son, Jonathan grew from being everybody's little brother to a solid-gold teen idol heartthrob.

Growing up on TV

Of course, one of the weird things about being a child star on a long-running sitcom is that you literally grow up in front of millions and millions of people. You can't hide certain things, like the onset of teenage acne or the squeaky break of a boy's voice change. Jonathan wasn't growing as tall and as fast as other kids his age. When he was twelve years old, the very mature-for-his-age actor told *16* magazine, "I realize that I'm smaller than other kids my age. Like, obviously *Home Improvement*'s older brother, Brad, played by Zachery Ty Bryan, is bigger than I am. He's really younger than I am, but I don't let that bother me. Actually, in the business that I'm in, acting, it helps me because I can play younger."

Even back then, Jonathan had a good attitude about something that often causes a lot of needless anxiety in preteens and teens. Continuing his conversation with *16*, Jonathan explained, "I don't mind being small. My dad's about six feet two. My mom's five feet five. My brother's five eleven — so obviously there's some height in my family. It just depends when I'm going to get it. The show has dealt with it. My character mentions his height. The director and I discussed this, and there was a lot of truth [in the episode]. At times I do say, man, I wish I was bigger. But I'm still very competitive in sports. I'm a good soccer player. I'm up there on my team, and it's just a matter of how you think about it. If you always dwell on it and say, 'Oh, I'm short. I'm never gonna be anything. I'm short so I can't play sports,' it's never gonna happen. But if you focus on something else, focus on kicking that soccer ball as hard as you can, on throwing a ball, you're gonna do the best you can. You're gonna have a very good performance.

"Sometimes I get teased, but the people who tease, I sometimes think, have no other words in their vocabulary. All they know how to do is tease. They can't have an intelligent conversation with anybody, so they just tease people. I just let it go in one ear and out the other. I don't really pay attention to it. Yeah, it's something that a lot of kids have to deal with. And I know that I'm gonna be taller when I'm older, and heck, if I'm not, no big deal."

"When I go home . . . I'm just Jonathan."

Three years and not much of a growth spurt later, Jonathan still had the same attitude about his height. He even showed a sense of humor about it. A *Movieline* interview with Jonathan was supposed to deal with his then-upcoming summer movie, *Wild America*. Instead, the conversation, which was taking place in a popular restaurant in the San Fernando Valley, was constantly interrupted by fans coming over and asking Jonathan for an autograph. One little boy came over to the booth where Jonathan and the reporter were sitting and said, as he motioned to a little girl at another table, "My cousin likes you, but she's scared of you."

"Scared?" Jonathan laughed. "I'm only five foot four. What's to be scared about?"

In another article, this time in *Seventeen*, Jonathan once again joked about his size. The writer had brought up his easygoing reputation, that you never hear about Jonathan Taylor Thomas throwing a temper tantrum. "I'm not one to toss my weight around — I'm only a hundred ten pounds," kidded the then-almost-sixteen-year-old.

During the late summer of 1998, Jonathan's personal growth made the news once again. No, there weren't headlines declaring how many inches Jonathan had grown. Instead, it was the announcement that even though he was probably the most popular teen on TV, he was cutting back his work schedule. In the 1998–1999 season of *Home Improvement*, Jonathan would only appear in three episodes, because he was determined to spend the year focused on school. Just as Jonathan turned seventeen, on September 8, 1998, he was entering his junior year in high school. "Colleges really look at your junior year," Jonathan explained in the press release. Though he's always been a straight-A student, Jonathan really wanted to concentrate on his education at this point. He's determined to get into a top school, perhaps even an Ivy League school like Harvard or Yale, and he wants to be prepared.

Those who really know Jonathan Taylor Thomas weren't surprised by his decision. The young superstar has always approached his career and his life with that kind of self-awareness and confidence. "The industry is neurotic and weird," Jonathan once observed to *Premiere*, "and so when I go home and I play basketball with my friends, I'm not Jonathan Taylor Thomas, I'm just Jonathan."

Just Jonathan — a young man who doesn't worry about the things he can't control but dedicates himself to the things he can. That makes Jonathan Taylor Thomas seem ten feet tall!

Chris O'Donnell (Batman and Robin)

"When I was sixteen, I was only 5'1" and weighed ninety-five pounds, so my options were limited to the shortest girls in school. I was totally worried, like, 'Man, when am I going to grow?'" [Twist]

Baby Spice (Emma Bunton)

"I'm not the thinnest of people, but that doesn't bother me. You've got to make the best of what you've got. Just put on your makeup and get out there and do it!" [People]

Minnie Driver (Good Will Hunting)

"When I was in high school, it was so vicious. If someone was a little overweight, people treated her differently. Now that I'm older I've learned that how you look is not so important. Besides, I don't want to look like everyone else. I want to be my own person." [Jump]

Brandy

As a freshman at Hollywood High Performing Arts, Brandy had trouble persuading a teacher to send her on auditions like other students. "One day I asked, 'Why aren't you sending me on calls?' And she said, 'Because you're not drop-dead gorgeous.' My heart just dropped." [People]

Paula Cole (singer/songwriter)

"I was the classic overachiever, getting straight A's, running for class president, trying so hard to be excellent and to please everybody. Then, [as I started maturing] I started feeling really uncomfortable with myself. I began hiding [my body] wearing really baggy clothes. [Eventually] I realized I was a repressed goody-two-shoes."

Paula's music is totally reflective of her growing-up angst. You hear it best in songs like "My Life" and "So Ordinary." She's psyched that those songs are being heard by teenage girls. "They're probably the people I want to touch the most. That was the hardest time in my life. I just want to let them know that those are the hardest times in many women's lives — that may help ease their burdens a bit." [Seventeen]

Cameron Diaz (There's Something About Mary)

"When I was growing up, I hated my body. I was extremely, extremely skinny as a child —

for years I was seventy-nine pounds, and much taller than everyone else. When I was in junior high, people thought I was sick. They used to call me Skeletor, or Skinny Bones Jones and all those other horrible names. I used to get into fights because I had to prove that if they pissed me off, I was going to kick their ass. My best girlfriend's mother told me years later she used to look at me and think, 'That poor child. What is she ever going to be able to do? She's so frail.'" [*Movieline*]

Jerry O'Connell (*Sliders*)

"'You were the little fat kid in *Stand By Me*.' That's what people usually say when they realize who I am. [But] I was never really fat. I was a chunky little kid. My mom gets upset when people say I was the fat kid." Jerry, who stands 6'3" and weighs 180 lbs., may be over it now, but he really was dissed for his weight back in those days. It had to hurt. When teen magazines interviewed the cast of *Stand By Me* — River Phoenix, Wil Wheaton, Corey Feldman — he was often left out, because the editors didn't think fans would like him: he was the fat one.

In school, he was often teased about it and tried to bluster his way through it. Jerry told a reporter, "Because I was husky, I remember challenging a girl in my class to punch me in the stomach, saying it wouldn't hurt because I was doing sit-ups and getting in shape. When she punched me, I farted!" In spite of that huge humiliation, Jerry really did start working out and by the time he hit his growth spurt, being the fat one was just a distant memory. [*Teen People*]

Scott Vickaryous (*Breaker High*)

"I was kind of skinny and short. I was teased all the time, so I had to learn to fend for myself. What happened was, I got a little loud; I

Sporty Spice
(Melanie Chisholm)
"In high school I was teased. They used to call me Holland, because Holland is so flat."
[*People*]

Drew Carey
(The Drew Carey Show)

"I hate being fat, desperately. I really want to lose weight. I weigh myself every morning and I hate it, hate it. I feel guilty all the time."
[NY Post]

Julianna Margulies
(ER)

"I was always teased for my fat head and big lips. I used to be called 'Flounder Mouth.'" [Movieline]

got a little mouthy. Which got me into more trouble. I realized you can't change the way you are — whether you're tall or really short, or however you're built. You have to learn to make the best of it — whatever body type you are. Whatever you want to do, just do it. . . . People were constantly telling me, 'you can't do that,' or 'you won't be good enough — you're too small.' What I tried to do was understand — that's their opinion, it doesn't have to be mine. I started to do the things I wanted to do. I started to do well at sports. I excelled at hockey, football, and I wrestled internationally. I did a lot of stuff. So I built up my body. I never did get big, but I did get in good shape. Mentally, as well as physically."

Rosie Perez (actress)

"I got teased because my body developed very quickly. So by the fifth grade, I was wearing a 34C bra, but I was only 4'9". . . . It was so humiliating because the boys used to make fun of me. In seventh grade, there was this one kid who used to run after me down the hallway and grab my breasts so hard, it hurt. Then, he'd make a honking noise. I started to hate my breasts because of it." [Movieline]

Shania Twain (singer/songwriter)

"I developed real young as a girl. I went through a lot of anger and frustration over that as a teenager. These guys see a girl who's developed up there, maybe they touch you up there and you really feel very invaded. And so, you know what? The easiest thing is to just cover them up, trying to get rid of the bounce factor. And that's what I did. I wore three shirts at a time. I tied myself in. And now I've got a song [on her album, Come On Over] called 'If You Want To Touch Her, Ask!' Well, it stems from that." [Rolling Stone]

Mia Tyler (model)

How would you feel if your dad was Aerosmith front man Steven Tyler, your way famous sister was model Liv Tyler — and you, at 5'7" and 145 lbs., became known as the "big girl" in a family of famous skinnies? A self-image disaster alert? Though there were times Mia Tyler, now 19, "lived on cottage cheese and melba toast," she eventually changed her attitude, not her dress size. "I looked in the mirror and decided I liked the way I look. I realized I just had to be myself. If I stay healthy and take care of myself, then I'm fine. Even better, I feel beautiful this way. I figure this is what I am — and that's the way it's gonna be." These days she's also a professional model for Lane Bryant plus-size fashions. In August 1998, Mia walked down the runway for Venezia Jeans. Dad Steven, sister Liv, and mom Cyrinda were on hand to cheer her on. [*People*]

Liv Tyler (*Armageddon*)

"I was a fat, ugly little girl. I still live in her body sometimes. I still feel ugly. Everyone has their moments."

Melissa Joan Hart
(*Sabrina the Teenage Witch*)

"It's tempting to think about going for a little liposuction, a chin extension. But when I was [posing for] the cover of *Details* magazine, with some of Hollywood's most beautiful women — Yasmine Bleeth, Carmen Electra, Alyssa Milano — they said they still feel insecure, no matter how good they look. I realized that having a perfect body or face doesn't automatically make you feel good about yourself." [*Seventeen*]

Sarah McLachlan
(singer/ songwriter)

"It took me a long time to get over the 'you're ugly and stupid' thing. From age thirteen to eighteen, it was consistent in my life, from my peers. You want desperately to fit in, and I tried hard, but I didn't." [*New York Post*]

81

Jennifer Aniston (*Friends*)

"In all shapes and sizes, people are absolutely beautiful. I didn't think I was overweight [as a young adult] until someone told me I was. I'd see thin bodies and think, 'That's beautiful, but that's not me.' Then I lost some weight — and I was still the same person."
[*All About You!*]

Fiona Apple (singer/songwriter)

"There were tough things about it, like there are tough things about anybody's childhood. I was very quiet. I was not great-looking. I wasn't aware of how I looked physically, so I didn't do anything to make myself pretty. All the kids thought I was a witch, and my teacher called me a cocker spaniel for a while because I had funny-looking hair. If you're different, sometimes people think you're weird. I think for a while I was very unhappy; I think it showed and people wanted to stay away from me."
[*New York Post*]

Michelle Williams (Dawson's Creek)

"I love food. I love to eat. I'm not going to give up eating to fit somebody else's conception of what beauty is." [People]

BRANDY

JAMES VAN DER BEEK

3

DANIELLE FISHEL

Jenny McCarthy

RELATIONSHIP
ISSUES

Claire Danes   "J"

JENNIFER LOVE HEWITT

Minnie Driver

NICHOLAS BRENDON

KATIE HOLMES

Jeremy London

Will Friedle

Bruce Springsteen once wrote, "Everybody has a hungry heart," meaning everybody wants to be loved, by a boyfriend, a girlfriend, a soulmate.

For lots of people, the starting gate to being loved opens with dating, and dating begins in high school, sometimes as early as junior high. It's usually, of course, the popular posse, the confident kids who hook up.

If you think your favorite stars fall into that category, you're in for a huge surprise. Some of today's most awesome stars are charter members of the "I've Been Dumped Club." Some of the hottest guys weren't such babe magnets back then; some didn't even score one date all through high school. Some are still singing the relationship blues in spite of all that fame and fortune.

If you want to be dating, but no one's reciprocating — take heart! You may feel very alone, but you have lots of company. Look around, and listen up.

BRANDY

"I WAS REALLY HEARTBROKEN. I WAS SICK, AND IT WAS HARD."

"Top of the World" is more than just a hit song for Brandy. It describes exactly how the versatile performer *should* be feeling right now. Professionally, this girl's got game — and she's on top of it.

Her pop duet with Monica, "The Boy Is Mine," shot to number one and stayed there for weeks. The shot was heard around the world as the song has charted globally. Brandy's second album, *Never S-A-Y Never*, which she executive-produced and cowrote, went multiplatinum within weeks of its release.

Her TV show *Moesha* is in its fourth hit season. She's especially proud that her TV special (with Whitney Houston) *Rodgers and Hammerstein's Cinderella* smashed viewing records *and* racial stereotypes. It's now on video.

Brandy's first movie, *I Still Know What You Did Last Summer*, is reaping big bucks at the box office; her personal reviews are solid.

And then there are the awards, which include numerous nominations for Grammys, MTV Video Awards, Lady of Soul Awards, and a stunning win in 1996 for the NAACP Image Newcomer Award.

She's modeling Candies footwear, the youngest pitchperson ever for that company, starring in her own Brandy comic book series, posing for the covers of national magazines *Seventeen, Vibe, Ebony,* and *TV Guide,* and even doing public service announcements on TV.

On *top* of being on top of the world, she's also naturally gorgeous, wealthy, and blessed with a supportive, protective family.

As her TV alter ego, Moesha, might put it, on the real, she *is* and she *has* all that. But on the real life train, none of that can shield her from a broken heart. "I have pain, just like everybody else," Brandy confessed. Lately, that pain has been caused by a broken relationship. Here's what happened, and how Brandy is coping.

The biggest fear: Never meeting a guy who'll love me for *me*

In addition to all her showbiz accomplishments, there's something else Brandy's famous for — not being allowed to date until the age of sixteen, and not being allowed to *seriously* one-on-one date until she turned eighteen. Back when she was a young teen, Brandy publicly balked at her parents' edict.

But as soon as she did reach the magic age of consent, she quickly realized her dating dilemmas went beyond the usual. As she expressed to a reporter, "It's hard to tell if a guy likes me for being Brandy the star, or just for me." When she heard the way another young star expressed it — "My biggest fear is that I'll never meet a guy who would actually love me for who I am" — Brandy wholeheartedly agreed with the sentiment. "That's the way I feel!" She added seriously, "That's why I'm not really interested in some of the guys who are interested in me. I don't know what their real purpose is." Then she joked, "Maybe I'll just stick to dating somebody that's a star, 'cause they'll understand."

That's exactly what she did. Unsurprisingly, the press, in one way or another, often tagged along.

Brandy and Kobe: "More didn't happen because he was so busy and I was so busy."

Because Brandy's a showbiz babe, she hasn't set foot in a regular high school classroom since ninth grade, but has been privately tutored instead. While she's well educated and even spent a semester at college, she did miss out on the extracurriculars like school sports, cheerleading, yearbooks, dances, and, of course, the prom. That was one reason she agreed to be basketball star Kobe Bryant's date for the senior prom when he graduated from Lower Merion High School in Ardmore, Pennsylvania.

For lots of reasons, the date was a major success.

Brandy had a ball just being in a normal high school situation. "It was so different for me to be around my peers because I didn't go to high school," Brandy gushed to *People* magazine. "The prom was so much fun. We had a wonderful time."

And she also really liked Kobe. Contrary to press reports, the prom date wasn't a career move, though it was heavily reported on and photographed. The real deal is that Brandy had met Kobe at an awards show, and the attraction was instant. "When I met him, I was, like, 'Oh, my God, you're cute!'" she admitted in *Ebony* magazine.

Kobe must have felt the same way. Brandy describes, "We had talked on the phone every day before the prom so we could get to know each other. He just seemed like a really, really nice person. So I asked my mom, and his mom talked with my mom."

The prom date between two teenage superstars was instant fodder for photographers and the gossip columns. The rumor mill had the two of them hooked up. It wasn't really true — but it could have been.

Rising sports hero Kobe wasn't into Brandy just because she was a star. He didn't need to be around her for publicity: he generated enough on his own, especially since he went pro (to the L.A. Lakers) right after graduation.

There *were* more dates between Brandy and Kobe, too. Unlike the prom, these were private, without benefit of photographers. As Brandy would later describe to *Seventeen* magazine, "I was out with Kobe, chillin', just doing normal teenage stuff."

But a real life romance between Brandy and Kobe never did get off the ground. "More didn't happen because he was so busy and I was so busy," she admitted. Brandy seemed disappointed, but not devastated.

Her first real brush with heartbreak was still to come.

Brandy and Usher: "I like his music."

Since the date with Kobe, Brandy has been linked to several other hot young superstars. But the names most frequently mentioned, Usher and Mase, are way off base. While she shared a TV romance with Usher — he played *Moesha* crush Jeremy — the two never dated off camera. "I like Usher's music, but don't tell him that," she giggled in an interview. "I don't want Usher to know that I like him. Usher is cool."

Brandy and Mase: "Not my type."

And as for twenty-year-old Mase, who is featured on her song "Top of the World," Brandy recalled first meeting him two years ago. "He asked, 'Can I marry you, girl?' And I was, like, 'Who are you?'"

Brandy's since found out, of course, and as she candidly told *TV Guide*, "He's not my type. He's my friend." Not that the friends haven't kicked it together. In *Seventeen*, she admitted, "He's taken me out a couple of times. He's shown me Harlem. We hang out a lot, but as far as a serious relationship goes, nope. But he's the sweetest guy. One time this bum came up to the car and said, 'Can you help me out?' Mase gave him a hundred dollars. I was so impressed."

Brandy and Wanya: "He was my first boyfriend."

The deep reason for Brandy's blues is Wanya Morris of Boyz II Men fame. Their relationship, carried on largely outside of the public eye, was the real deal. And though she's done talking about it, Brandy publicly aired her grief back when it was freshest.

She met Wanya in 1995 when she, supporting her first album, was touring with Boyz II Men. They became instant buds and after the tour ended, talked on the phone every day. Publicly, Brandy confessed, "I've had a crush on him since I was sixteen. I got goo-goo eyed."

She described, "For so long I was his best friend. He was like a brother, I was like his little sister. I don't think he liked me [romantically] when I was a young girl. But I, like, grew up right in front of him. I grew up in his eyes."

In 1997, Brandy invited Wanya to her star-studded eighteenth birthday party at Hollywood's House of Blues. The bash was photographed and recorded in *People* magazine. "It's a party honoring a beautiful person," Wanya had told reporters, adding, "she has been kept on a short leash by her folks. Brandy should start dating."

What he *didn't* say was *who* she should be dating. That turned out to be him. "We finally got together when I was of age," Brandy has admitted. "It was very private."

The relationship lasted eighteen months. And then it fell apart. "We were always not together," she explained in *People* magazine. "It was hard. . . . We figured it was better for us to be friends."

In describing the breakup, Brandy has revealed that *she* ended it. Every time she talked about it, she teared up. At first she implied that the split was temporary. "We're not together," she told *US*. "We're going through a phase of taking space."

In later interviews, she confessed that the breakup was permanent. And heartbreaking. "I've gone through that, you know, breaking up with him, my first love. I was really heartbroken. I was sick, and it was hard, really hard, but I got through it. I'm okay now. I miss him, but I'm okay. He's [in my heart] always. He's special to me. But we had to move on . . . whoever he ends up with will be happy."

"I want somebody to hug me and say, 'Brandy, I'm glad you're in my life, and I love you.'"

Coping for Brandy means being very cautious about jumping into another relationship. "I'm so single right now," she told *TV Guide*. "It's better that way." It also means throwing herself into her work — and allowing her pain to be expressed in her music. Check it: Six of the songs she cowrote on *Never S-A-Y Never* were inspired by her romance and bustup with Wanya.

As soon as the album was finished, she hopped a plane for Mexico to film her first movie, *I Still Know What You Did Last Summer*. Without a break, she threw herself into the Candies campaign, a seemingly endless round of interviews and photo sessions to promote her projects — and of course, the new season of *Moesha*. Through it all, she slapped on a happy face and assured her public she was fine — better than fine. "This is the life I've always wanted. I'm happy about it," she burbled in *People* magazine.

Is Brandy over her heartbreak? She's getting there. "I will never get down on myself because of a guy," she said, adding, "never let a guy be your sole focus — that only gets you in trouble. If something doesn't work out, just try to learn from it and move ahead."

Yet moving ahead, keeping busy, and keeping focused doesn't mean Brandy has given up on love. In *Ebony*, she spilled her true heart. "I want somebody to hug me and say, 'Brandy, you're cute, and I'm glad you're in my life, and I love you,' and all that. But it's hard to find that person."

DANIELLE FISHEL

Danielle Fishel must have a lot of self-confidence. Like, when Danielle was twelve and was first cast in the TV series *Boy Meets World*, she was slated for a minor role. But even as an almost-extra, Danielle stole the show. The producers were so impressed, they changed their minds and decided to make her a central character. So in one afternoon, Danielle became Topanga, the veggie-loving, always politically correct flower child.

Those who know Danielle weren't surprised by this on-the-spot promotion. Ever since she could first express what was on her mind, Danielle has set goals for herself — and, most of the time, achieved them. She isn't pushy or overbearing about it. The seventeen-year-old just looks at a situation, assesses the pros and cons, and acts accordingly.

Danielle learned this levelheaded approach to life from her parents, Rick, an executive at a medical equipment company, and Jennifer, Danielle's manager. So it's not surprising friends would seek out Danielle for advice. Danielle's keep-to-the-basics attitude makes her a good problem solver. Most important, she's not a "do what I say, not what I do" confidante. Danielle follows her *own* advice, especially when it comes to dating and relationships. In an interview with *Teen Beat*, Danielle was asked to give her dating tips. Instead of a list of dos and don'ts, Danielle got right to the heart of the matter. She said, "Well, if you're going to have a relationship with someone, I think communication is very important. Just be cool, and you have to let the other person have their freedom. I'm a very independent person, and I kind of feel trapped if someone tries to control anything I'm doing. So give the other person their freedom and don't be a jealous person."

"He grabbed me by the arm and spun me around."

Danielle definitely knows about jealousy in a controlling relationship firsthand. Here's her story.

It's about a boy she had dated when she was in tenth grade. It was during the spring, when *Boy Meets World* goes on hiatus. During the shooting season of her series, Danielle takes classes with a tutor on the set, but once the show wraps, she heads right back to regular school and her friends. Things were great. Danielle was glad to be back hanging out with her classmates, and she had just started dating a hottie.

"We'd only been together for three weeks," she recalls. "It was a really new relationship. One day at school, I was talking to a good friend who happens to be a guy. I hadn't seen him for a few months, because he had graduated. He had come back for a visit.

We were having a really great time talking, and all of a sudden my boyfriend came over, grabbed me by the arm, spun me around, and said, 'What are you doing?'

"'I'm talking to Matt,' I said. And he was, like, 'You should not be over here talking. You're my girlfriend, and all my friends want to know what my girlfriend is doing talking to another guy.'

"He tried to drag me away, and I'm, like, 'Excuse me?!!!! You can tell your friends that if they have a problem, they're not part of our relationship. And if it's you who has the problem, you can turn around and say bye right now, because I want to talk to Matt.'

"So he did, and we broke up."

Danielle said that she never had a clue her new boyfriend was that possessive. His caveman attitude came right out of the blue. "It just happened," she says. "Everything was great up until then, and then suddenly there was this control he had to have over me: 'You're my girlfriend!' I was, like, 'Uh, no, I'm not. Go away!'"

Right then and there Danielle knew that if she stopped talking to her friend Matt and followed her boyfriend over to his buddies, she would be in deep trouble. If she allowed it to happen once, Danielle knew it would happen again . . . and again. As a matter of fact, Danielle was aware that if she permitted him to get away with such bullish behavior, there was a chance that she could find herself in a seriously dangerous situation. Because Danielle has respect for herself, she expects respect from her friends and especially someone she dates. It doesn't matter if the boy is the captain of the football team, the studmuffin of the class, or the boy next door, he has no right to treat anyone as a possession.

Breaking up is hard to do

Sometimes it's surprisingly hard to break up with someone who isn't treating you with respect. Sometimes you think you'll never get another date if you call it quits. Sometimes you stay in a bad relationship out of habit or a false sense of security. Sometimes you think, "He will change," or "If I just try harder, she will be nice to me." Usually that's a trap.

And Danielle decided early on no one was going to have that kind of control over her. That attitude and self-confidence are not only good for her but are an example to others. As she told a friend, "Whether girls believe it or not, there are guys out there who do want to treat girls like ladies and will respect you for who you are. So don't stick with one who won't, because you'll find someone ten times better."

NICHOLAS BRENDON

"I NEVER DATED AT ALL."

On TV's *Buffy the Vampire Slayer*, he plays Alexander Harris, but everyone calls him Xander. Off camera, he's Nicholas Brendon, but his friends know him as Nicky.

Nicky makes friends frequently and easily. He's as outgoing, un-affected, easy to talk to and to get to know . . . as, well, Xander.

Obviously, Xander doesn't get how cute and attractive he is. Mostly he considers himself a flop with girls, even when the evidence is totally to the contrary. In season one he had an unrequited crush on Buffy, but at the same time he was Willow's not-so-secret crush object. But season two found him actually getting the girl — the most unlikely of all, snobby, catty Cordelia, the rich in-crowd babe who'd only talk to him one way: down. But eventually even she couldn't help being drawn to Xander's offbeat appeal.

To the actor who plays him, it's sweet irony that Xander has become a babe magnet *and* a quipmeister. In his real life high school years, neither could be further from his experience. Nicky never dated. And when he was nervous, the boy could barely speak.

"I had a horrible stutter."

Nicholas Brendon grew up in Grenada Hills, California, with his parents and twin brother, Kelly. Nicky remembers a fairly normal childhood. He went to public school, played Little League, and occasionally got into twin trouble trying to fool teachers by switching classes with his brother.

Even though his mom worked sporadically as a theatrical agent, he never considered a career in acting. If Nicky had a "when I grow up" goal, it was a toss between pro baseball and medicine. Showbiz was not in the equation.

Which isn't to say Nicky didn't love making people laugh. Entertaining others gave him a kick. The kick grew into a passion as he grew older. "I was starting to feel the *need* to somehow entertain people," he admitted in an interview. With increasing frequency, he'd try jokes out on his family, say outrageous things just to get a reaction — and it worked. He found he really had a knack for it.

But the idea of a career in comedy or acting was too terrifying to even contemplate back then. He related in an interview, "When I was alone with my family, I was fine. I was funny and things were great. It was when I was out in the world . . . well, people are very judgmental."

Nicky's toughest time, when he felt people judged him harshly, was in high school. "It was a horrible experience," he admitted during a *Buffy* press conference. He went to Chatsworth High, part of the Los Angeles Unified system, where one of his schoolmates was Leonardo DiCaprio. But where Leo was a class clown, Nicky was the opposite.

He revealed the reasons in *YM* and followed up with another reporter. "In junior high, when my gawky stage hit, it hit hard.

When I was in high school, I was so insecure, I wouldn't even talk to people. I had a stutter — a horrible stutter that made talking to people hard and talking in front of people impossible."

"People," of course, included girls. "I never dated at all," Nicky confessed. "I was too shy. At one point, I was really into this good friend of mine, but I was too shy to tell her."

Things seemed to slide further downhill during that time and just after those rough high school years. He didn't feel he was good-looking; zits seemed to pop up at the worst possible times. He fractured his elbow and quit baseball. His studies weren't going so well — the early dream of medicine was becoming ever more distant.

And then his parents broke up.

The turning point: Let's deal with this

In a strange and circuitous way, however, dealing with all the bad stuff is what brought him to the happiest time in his life. Facing things head on — and a talk with God — is what led him to overcome the stutter, to feel confident enough to ask a girl out, and ultimately, to the career he loves and is now flourishing in.

There's no trace of the wisecracking Xander when Nicky tells of the moment that changed his life.

"I was sitting in the backyard of our old house. It was summertime, really beautiful, the end of the day with the sun going down. The Dodgers were playing, I had the radio on in the background. And it all hit me. My parents were getting divorced. High school was almost over. What was I going to do? Not baseball, because I quit. And I was just talking to God, and I said, 'What can I do?'"

Two thoughts came to him. One, he loved entertaining

people — even if it was only in the privacy of his own home, among family who accepted him. And two, he wanted to help his mother out financially. Showbiz seemed like a path.

But there was the stutter. He couldn't even talk to girls. How could he audition for parts, act out a scene, be funny? At this point, most people would have succumbed to that sinking feeling and said, "Forget it. I can't." But Nicky Brendon isn't most people. In a moment of clarity, and not without a lot of courage, he made a decision. "I just came to this conclusion that when I'm forty, I don't want to say, 'I wish I had done that.' So I said, 'You know what? Let's do it.'"

By "let's do it," he meant let's work on eliminating the stutter, the one thing that was holding him back. "It was very hard," Nicky admitted in an interview. "I didn't go to a speech therapist. I just did a lot of tongue twisters. I slowed down my speech a lot. It was a lot of hard work. I was happy I did it, though."

Understatement alert. Overcoming the stutter was the start. It gave him confidence to try out for roles and to interact with people. Including girls.

Nicholas Brendon's high school days are way behind him. Over the course of those years, he's made up for lost time socially. Although he's neither seeing nor crushing on any of his female costars, in interviews he's revealed that he has dated much and has even been in a few serious relationships.

In spite of that, Nicky insists that sometimes he feels as insecure as he did as a young teenager. "I don't see myself as being cute or hot," he revealed, adding, "I get tongue-tied when I talk to a girl I like. I'm all jittery and I say stupid things, which pretty much ensures I'll never date her!"

In interviews, too, traces of the old stutter are still apparent.

"If you *want* to do it, you've *got* to do it."

"I want to inspire people." That's one of Nicky's lifetime goals. "I want people to say, 'Nicholas Brendon, he's supposedly the nicest guy in the world.' I want to do good work, but more than that, I want to stay a good human being. That's more important than any character I play."

Nicky has a message for fans that comes from his own life experience. "I just kind of developed my sense of humor through a life full of ups and downs. You just have to learn to laugh at life and not take it so seriously. Never lose the inner child in you. And remember, there's nothing that you can't do. If you *want* to do it, you've *got* to do it."

JAMES VAN DER BEEK

"I'M A DORK. I'M DEFINITELY NOT OUTGOING."

If *Dawson's Creek* is the breakout teen TV show of the recent season, its star, James Van Der Beek, is the "it" boy, the boy with the buzz. Blond, crush-worthy, and disarmingly charming, James is one of TV's brightest young stars. Soon after his *Dawson* debut, he vaulted onto the covers of national magazines from *YM* to *TV Guide* to *Teen People* to *People* magazine's 50 Most Beautiful. The offers come pouring in daily to appear on talk shows, to make big-money promotional appearances, to star in movies.

This is now. What about then? Well, in many ways, it seems as if James was just born perfect, popular, and on the success track. Articles about his growing-up years usually mention his loving, secure home life and well-rounded school résumé. The boy was a promising athlete, a talented drama dude, *and* a major brainiac, a National Honor Society member who earned academic scholarships to prep school and to college. As expressed by one reporter, he was good at everything — to which James conceded, "Kind of enough to make you puke." Or, as his TV best bud Joey put it in the show's first season, "Accept your perfect life, Dawson."

But as the fictional TV season unfolded, that "perfection" crumbled like a kicked-over sand castle. In real life, too, James hasn't had it quite so smooth.

Superficial interviews aside, a scratch beneath the surface reveals a boy who wasn't so confident, who endured the taunts of a bully, who never felt he was cool — who sometimes felt like a loser with girls.

James slips into Dawson's skin so easily because he identifies big time. "I call Dawson the dork in all of us," he once mused. "He's not really, really cool, and he's not part of the in crowd. He's . . . different. He's a warped version of me at fifteen. Now, at twenty-one, most of the adolescent wounds are still very fresh — I get to relive all the tragedy and the heartbreak." Okay, but if Dawson's romantic life is complicated, at least he has one. James mostly didn't.

"She wound up with some other guy — right in front of me."

James is the oldest of three kids. His dad, a former minor league baseball player, worked for the telephone company. His mom, a former dancer, was a gym teacher and gymnastics studio owner. The Van Der Beeks weren't quite as well off as the fictional Leerys appear to be; they lived in what James terms "a modest little split-level house" in suburban Cheshire, Connecticut.

The boy's early dreams weren't so modest. Just as his parents were athletic, so was James, who dreamed of a career in pro sports. Every year he tried out for the school football team, and every year he won a starting position. He thought he had a good shot at going pro. In fact, as a child, James's self-image — due to his natural abilities and loving, supportive family — was pretty solid.

Until junior high, that is. That's when everything changed. "It was funny," he shared with a reporter. "In eighth grade, we were asked to write a letter to ourselves about where we would be in five years. I wrote that I wanted to be a pro baseball player like my father or a physical therapist."

But soon after that essay got handed in, James's jock dreams went buh-bye. That's when, trying to catch a pass in football practice, he fell and suffered a concussion. Doctor's orders: no football, no sports that year.

To fill his suddenly free time, James tried out for the school play. Experience-free, still he won the starring role of Danny Zuko in *Grease*. Immediately he got hooked on acting and tried out for plays in community theater. From that point on, James's feelings about acting mirrored Dawson's about filmmaking: It became his focus, his passion, and maybe his obsession. On-line, he said, "Dawson and I were both very impassioned at an early age. Dawson is a burgeoning filmmaker whose overactive imagination and idealism sometimes make him oblivious. He's prone to rejecting reality for a more romantic scenario. He's a bit of an innocent and is frequently off in his own little world." James added, "All of which I can definitely relate to."

As he noted in his *Interview* magazine cover story, "In *Grease*, I got to be the cool guy, who I never was in school. Acting was so inspiring and exciting, because to me it was play — make-believe." And make-believe could be way more fun than real life.

Pursuing acting didn't win him popularity points with the kids at school. Once he decided to go for it, he'd make frequent three-hour trips into New York for auditions. Aside from snaring the interest of a professional manager quickly, roles did not come regularly. Rejection was the most common result of James's auditions. Every once in a while, however, he did nail down a part.

Not that the kids at school cared one way or the other. "It was absolutely impossible [to share what I was going through]. There was no way I could talk to anybody at school about it," James told a reporter.

Anybody, of course, included girls.

"I didn't date a lot," he admitted. "There was definitely a real life Joey, a girl who was a friend but wasn't a girlfriend." There were, instead, zits and bullies (a football teammate of James's brother used to give him flack) and on one unforgettable occasion, heinous humiliation. He admitted in a magazine, "I went to a homecoming dance with a girl who was trying to break up with me. But she said, 'I still really want to go to homecoming with you.' So I went, thinking I was gonna win her back. It was just terrible. It was her high school, so I barely knew anybody else. And she wound up with some other guy — right in front of me."

Ego-smasher alert. But perhaps this was worse: Right around the same time, James's drama teacher at Cheshire Academy, the boarding school he attended as a day student, blithely informed him that he didn't have enough acting talent for anything more professional than community theater.

As his high school years progressed, James felt like more of an outsider than ever. He'd gone from public school to the private Cheshire Academy (through a scholarship) and found the adjustment tough. "I was kind of blown away by what I was seeing there," he admitted. And although he was back to playing school sports, the combination of athletics and theater made him an outsider. "The two worlds didn't exactly overlap," he said.

His interests weren't like those of his peers; his taste in music wasn't the same as everyone else's. "Other kids were listening to the radio, and I was going to the library and getting [Broadway] cast albums of plays. I was doing all the community theater I could. I put up walls. I was in my own head, kind of a loner." He added, "At that point, my goal in high school was just surviving it intact."

The turning point: A teacher who "made me feel valuable for being different."

Because he felt he couldn't talk to his friends about what was really going on in his life, James turned to writing. "To express how I was feeling, I would write stories," he told *Interview*. "[I was] encouraged by my English teacher. To this day, I consider that teacher a mentor. He made me feel valuable for being different."

And that, all by itself, gave James the courage to stick to his passions, even when it distanced him from his peers — and in spite of the diss by his drama teacher. And when the role of Dawson Leery came his way, everything came together. "This is the first time I've ever been in the right place at the right time at the right age in my life," he announced triumphantly.

"I don't feel different, but I'm being treated differently."

Because he's Dawson, because he's a star, James gets a totally different reaction from his peers — and from girls — these days. He is sought after, admired, he is the man! He is . . . confused. The first time he saw himself on a billboard, he burst out laughing at the absurdity of it all. "I didn't know how to deal with the hype. I keep asking myself, 'How did I get there?' I don't see how someone could get a big ego out of [this], because it's not you."

The fan adoration doesn't feel real. As he relayed in *Entertainment Weekly* about a personal appearance, "There were five thousand screaming teenage girls going, 'Oh, my God, you rock! You're hot! I love you!' I've never felt more detached from a group of people in my life." When he and Josh Jackson were at a *Seventeen* magazine party, tossing souvenir T-shirts to the crowd, "We walked out and everybody went nuts. I was like a deer in the headlights. I didn't know how to react."

Being an idolized TV and movie star hasn't made his social life much easier. James revealed, "Dawson is a tragically nice guy — and so am I. I'm still nervous and shy when I meet girls. The only thing that's changed is that I get to meet more girls now because they introduce themselves to me."

In true Dawson style, there might be a special someone in his life. He's just not sure where it's going.

KATIE HOLMES

Joey Potter of *Dawson's Creek* is the role of a lifetime — at least nineteen-year-old Katie Holmes thinks so. "She is a fifteen-year-old girl [who] uses a tough attitude as a guard because she's been through so much," Katie is quoted in her *Dawson's Creek* press bio. "She's been hurt so many times that she doesn't want to be vulnerable and put herself out there for everyone. She has to be tough."

Indeed, Joey has had to handle more problems than Mother Love does on a week of *Forgive or Forget* shows. There are some who feel Joey should have a direct dial connection to Dr. Joyce Brothers!

But Joey is hardly someone to be pitied. From the start, Katie was determined to explore all sides of Joey. "Because of the way my character looks and acts, people perceive her as just a one-dimensional trashy girl from the other side of the tracks," Katie explained to the *New York Daily News*. "She has her dreams like everybody."

Because she admires Joey's spirit, Katie admitted to *US* magazine, "I'm actually working on becoming more like her. She's so smart and strong. And witty."

Indeed Joey does have a lot of qualities that Katie appreciates. Comparing herself with Joey, Katie confessed to *Teen Beat* magazine, "I'm shy at first. Joey's not shy, and she tells things like they are. She doesn't hold back. I kind of hold things in — I don't say certain things. We're different. She's more of a tomboy. She says things I probably wouldn't say. She's sweet deep down, but she says things out of jealousy and hurt feelings. She's rough around the edges, and I'm more laid-back."

Part of the reason Katie can handle emotions a bit better than Joey is because of her upbringing. Katie is the youngest of five children. She grew up in a warm, loving, two-parent home in Toledo, Ohio. Katie was encouraged by her parents to try new things, to take chances. Sometimes it didn't work out, but Katie never considered herself a failure — she just looked around for something else to try.

A perfect example of Katie picking herself up and moving on was when she decided she was going to be the next Rebecca Lobo. At five feet seven inches, Katie was taller than most girls in her high school, so it was natural she was encouraged to try out for sports. "I come from a superathletic family," she told *Jump*. "I attempted to play basketball and softball, *attempted* being the key word here. The truth is, I was horrible at sports. I realized it just wasn't my thing, but I had to do *something*. So I tried going out for parts in the musicals at my school."

"I wanted to be an actress, but I'm from Ohio."

That's when Katie found her natural talent. She was a born actress. She appeared in school play after school play. The irony was that although Katie seemed to come alive when she was onstage, the shy side of her almost kept her from totally pursuing her dream. "I wanted to be an actress, but I'm from Ohio," she explained in a very candid interview with *Seventeen*. "I told myself, 'Get a grip.'"

Katie was surprised when things started working out. When she was sixteen, she went to a modeling and talent convention in New York City. There she met a talent agent who encouraged her to go to Los Angeles for the next TV pilot season. Screwing up all her courage, Katie flew out to Hollywood. It was a good news–bad news trip. The bad news was that Katie didn't get a TV series, but the good news was that on her first audition, she was cast in the movie *The Ice Storm*. Her costars were Elijah Wood, Christina Ricci, and Tobey Maguire. Working with actors of this quality was a major coup for Katie. It was as if her first time in front of the camera was like taking grad-school courses before even finishing acting class 101. Pretty good for a little girl from Toledo, Ohio.

After *The Ice Storm*, Katie returned to Toledo to resume high school. When she was asked to audition for a new TV drama called *Dawson's Creek*, she was beyond excited. Until she realized that the Los Angeles audition conflicted with her senior class production of *Damn Yankees*. She was playing the lead, Lola, and Katie wasn't about to disappoint her classmates and skip out on them. Luckily, the *Dawson's Creek* producers were able to reschedule, and Katie won the role of Joey. Katie somehow knew that because winning the role of Joey against all odds, it was definitely meant to be.

"Only a few girls get to be prom queens and get all the guys."

When Katie read the first *Dawson's Creek* script, she immediately bonded with Joey. Even though her real life experiences were nothing like the character's. Still, there *was* something Katie connected with: the pain of unrequited love — worse yet, of not having her affections even noticed! "I was never the kind of girl who got a lot of attention from guys, so I can relate to the trauma of liking somebody and not having him like you back," Katie said when she discussed Joey with a *Jump* magazine writer. As impossible as it may have seemed, the writer felt Katie knew what she was talking about — from personal experience.

It was obvious that Katie spoke from the heart when she continued that line of thought with *Seventeen*. "Only a few girls get to be prom queens and get all the guys. Those girls are like Jen. Joey isn't the girl who gets all the guys. I wasn't like that, either, so I can relate."

Not only could Katie relate, but more important she knew that not being the prom queen type was hardly a fatal flaw. When Katie wasn't asked to a school dance or football game, she didn't lock herself in her bedroom and cry "poor me." Instead she did something else she enjoyed, whether it was going to the movies with friends, working on a new play, or going to the event with a group of friends who didn't have dates, either. What Katie learned back in high school — and maybe will teach Joey — is that all things come with time. When she was a laughing disaster on the basketball court, she didn't give up and hide in embarrassment. She did a little soul-searching and discovered her real talent, acting. And she became the school star. When she questioned whether a Midwestern girl could make it in Hollywood, she screwed up her courage and went for it. And she became a professional actress. The next thing on Katie's agenda is to find that true-blue soul mate — if she could only find the time!

Jennifer Love Hewitt
(*Party of Five*)

"[I have had a broken heart.] You can't breathe, your eyes are pouring a thousand tears a second and you can't foresee going on [with love] because you never want to feel this way again. But then you have to look in the mirror and say, 'Shut up, eat some ice cream, be by yourself for a while and think about who you are and who you want to be — then, go out and find someone compatible. A broken heart feels like the worst thing in the whole world, but it really helps you decide what you want and don't want. You learn a lot from a broken heart." [*Teen*]

"J"
(Five)

"My first girlfriend and I used to argue all the time. If I got annoyed, I'd tell her it was over and storm out of the house. Then she'd follow me and we'd make up. It was always me ending it. But a week before my eighteenth birthday, my girlfriend ended it. When I called her to make up, she really stuck to her guns and didn't want to get back together. It really, really killed me because I'd been with her for four years. [But] we were arguing too much and she couldn't take it anymore. You know all those times when you say it's over, but you know deep in your heart, it isn't? There comes a time when you just know. You say it's over and you actually mean it. I [still] have a soft spot in my heart for my ex, but we both knew it wouldn't work out if we got back together."

Claire Danes
(Romeo + Juliet)

"When somebody dumps you, however and in what way, it's traumatic and tragic. The feelings are so volatile. When your romantic life goes away, it completely changes how you look at the world." [New York Post]

Jeremy London
(Party of Five)

"I got dumped by my fiancée. It's depressing. She dumped me out of the blue. She didn't even give me my ring back. It made me feel really bad about myself. I thought I was going to be with her for the rest of my life." [*Sassy*]

Jenny McCarthy
(entertainer)

"After a breakup, I just keep in mind that there are so many other fish in the sea and that somebody better is on the way." [*YM*]

Will Friedle
(Boy Meets World)

Will was blind-sided when he got dumped by Jennifer Love Hewitt — he never saw it coming. It still hurts to talk about it.

Minnie Driver

The only thing worse than being dumped by Matt Damon was having the whole world find out that he left her: Matt [who'd previously busted up with Claire Danes!] announced the breakup on *Oprah*. Ouch.

MELISSA JOAN HART

USHER

FAMILY ISSUES

WILSON CRUZ

WILL FRIEDLE

KATE WINSLET

MONICA

HARVEY SILVER

LeAnn Rimes

You can choose your friends but not your family. So goes the old cliché. But just like you can't choose your friendship issues, you totally have no control over family strife.

Best-case scenario goes like this: The people we're related to are the ones we go to for comfort, support. We connect with kin when the rest of the world seems hostile. Within our family, we are free to be ourselves, to have bad mood days, say hurtful stuff, get it off our chests. We *know* we'll always be forgiven.

But the best-case scenario isn't always the real deal. Sometimes those family ties are the ones that bind and choke.

Anyone who's got a family has got family issues. Some can be as common as sibling rivalry; others are more dramatic, leave more scars. The stories of the next four celebs cover all the bases.

Each story in this section will move you; hopefully, one will inspire you.

MELISSA
JOAN HART

Melissa Joan Hart has it all together. Well, that's her image, anyway. Mostly, it's the characters she's played. She's still known all over the world as Nickelodeon's Clarissa, who had all the answers and "Explained It All" to an audience of millions each week.

Now, she's Sabrina, the Teenage Witch, who may not know it all, but who could — if she chose — make all her issues disappear with a flick of her finger.

"My fans still think I have the answers to everything," she concedes.

The TV image isn't too far from the real-life Melissa. She is a totally upbeat young woman who believes in tackling her issues head on, by talking them through. Though at twenty-two, she's been through it all — friendships, relationships, school stuff — the issue she's most experienced in is the family thing. Specifically, sibling stuff. She ought to be: Melissa's got six sisters and a brother. What's it like to grow up in such a huge brood? As she relates, there have been some amazing times, and there have been some sucky ones as well.

If you thought being from a big family was all fun and games, you might be in for a surprise. And if you are one among several sibs, maybe you'll relate to some of what Melissa went through.

The upside: "I have built-in best friends."

"I'm the firstborn in our family; in April 1999, I'll be twenty-three. After me comes Trisha, who's twenty-one; Elizabeth, eighteen; Brian, fifteen; and Emily, thirteen. Our more recent arrivals — after my mom remarried — are Alexandra Hart-Gilliams, five, and Samantha, who was born in November 1997. Since I've always been the oldest, it's hard to imagine life any other way. It was always a thrill whenever a new baby arrived, always having another one to play with.

"I never wished to have fewer siblings. I actually thought having such a large family was normal. I grew up in a small town with a large percentage of Catholic families — everyone had a lot of kids. I mean, families with seven or eight kids weren't uncommon. I had one friend who was an only child. The only thing I was envious of, was that she got to be closer with her parents than I could — she was almost like a friend to them. But otherwise, I felt sorry for her. She must have been lonely. I *never* was!

"I especially loved having so many sisters and my brother when we'd go on vacation. We drove to Florida a lot, and I always had someone to do stuff with. Like, if I wanted to go down to the pool, I never had to go alone. There was always someone willing to go.

"For the most part, I had built-in best friends. We ate together every night, and at bedtime, it was like having nightly sleepovers. Sometimes we even pushed the beds next to each other, so we could all sleep together, because we were scared of everything — we were such wimps! We'd check under the beds, and behind the closet doors, and make sure the hall light was on and the door was open just the right amount. Lots of kids are scared of the dark, scared to go to sleep; we were lucky that we had each other to be scared with!

"Of course, there were fights. But the wonderful thing about growing up in a large family is that whenever you get into fights, you have teams. It's more like we're debating than fighting; and it makes the conflicts less personal, because when you're all in it together, it's more about what's right than about hurting someone's feelings.

"And because there are so many of us, there's always someone to protect you, and the sides are always changing. I usually protect Emily because she's the youngest of the bigger kids, and everyone picks on her. That's another thing about big families — we all look out for one another.

"We bickered sometimes over clothes, but not that much. Most of the time, we all got our own new stuff — except for Elizabeth, who got all the hand-me-downs. The only 'clothes-encounters' I remember was when someone would 'borrow' something of mine without asking. Actually, they still do! Now that I have my own place, I have to search them before they leave — make sure they haven't absconded with any of my stuff. The truth is, I never really minded that much, except when they took something that didn't even belong to me, that I'd borrowed from a friend. That's when it became complicated. To this day, when I can't find something, I'm quick to accuse one of my sisters of taking it, before I really know if it's true."

The downside: "I've always been a sharing person — I never had a choice."

"Of course, the thing with best friends is that you always have that best friend/worst enemy dynamic happening. The competition between kids closest in age is usually the most intense, and that was true of me and Trisha. In the beginning, we both started out in showbiz together, so we were both auditioning. That made the competition worse. It was her decision to quit. And to this day, she's the only one in the family who doesn't act. Instead, she was able to have the most normal schooling — she's in college now — and probably the most normal social life.

"Things became difficult right after my parents' divorce. Before that, we lived in a house in the suburbs. Afterward, my mom and five of us moved to a small apartment in New York City. I've always been a sharing person — clothes, toys, rooms — I never had a choice. And I didn't know about privacy, growing up — it wasn't an option. All that intensified when we moved.

"In that apartment, we all had to share one bathroom — it was so small you could brush your teeth, use the toilet, and take a shower all at the same time! That bathroom was the most coveted room in the apartment, not only for obvious reasons, but because it was the only room with a lock. So there was always someone in there, and always someone banging on it to get in.

"Trish and I clashed over our bedroom, which we shared. It was small to begin with, and we'd fight over space. I admit I took most of it. Our styles were so different! Her side of the room was all Laura Ashley; on my side, I put the mattress on the floor, painted the walls with bright designs, and had all these long 'Clarissa' necklaces hanging all over the place.

"Naturally, we fought over everything having to do with that room — who was being too loud, whose music was better, when to shut the light for bedtime. We'd 'resolve' our differences by yelling at each other — or by running to our mom.

"There was one really intense fight we had. Now, we laughingly refer to it as 'the family embarrassment.' We were all in a nice restaurant in Los Angeles, at a corner table. I guess there was some tension betweeen me and Trisha, becaue she was trying to get a stray eyelash off my face, and pinched me deliberately. So I punched her!

"But looking back, I have to say that it was really in our preteen years that Trish and I defined our differences and kind of ignored each other a lot. It was almost as if we purposely didn't want to mix our lifestyles."

"There are people who'll always be there for me."

"Sometimes in big families, the parents sort of give each kid an identity — but we did it ourselves. I'm the creative one; Trisha is the intelligent one; Brian is the athlete; Emily the cute one. Then there's Elizabeth, who was the middle child for a long time. She used to be the quiet one — I mean, I don't remember her talking when she was a kid — and the one who was pushed around sometimes. It was almost as if she said, 'Hey, wait, I need to stand out, and be different.' And when she turned fifteen, she suddenly got loud! Anyway, she's great at drawing, arts and crafts, painting, so she's now the artistic one. As for the babies, well, we're not sure about them yet.

"One thing we all learned early on was to speak up for ourselves. No one holds his or her feelings in, everyone's up front. Even when rude things are said, you always know what the deal is and can start resolving things. One tactic we use now is to just take a 'time out,' walk away from a conflict. It isn't easy, but that's what we do. Most of the time, when we cool off and return, we end up laughing about it later. Being very open with each other is another bonus of having such a large family. I'm not afraid to do anything in front of my brother and sisters.

"Because of *Clarissa Explains It All*, and now *Sabrina*, I've been the most well-known one in the family. Which has been a mixed bag, to say the least!

"For the most part, my siblings have not been jealous, instead, they've been very proud. And I never felt guilty about it, because there was a time, after my parents split up, that we had no money. And, because I'd just gotten the part of Clarissa, I was the one supporting the family. Don't get me wrong, I would have taken the role anyway, no matter what our circumstances had been. But there was a little extra pressure on me in those days. I mean, I couldn't let my family go without while I was making money. Luckily, that situation didn't last very long. My mom and I formed a production company, Hartbreak Films, my brother and sisters were acting, my mom remarried, and things got better pretty quickly.

"Some of my younger siblings would 'use' the fact that Clarissa was their sister to make friends at school. That bugged me, so I told them to stop. And there was Trisha, who used to be embarrassed that I was Clarissa. We look enough alike so people were always questioning her, and eventually she got over it. Now, Trisha's thrilled at the way things have worked out. She's glad she's not in showbiz. And the truth is, there were times I was jealous of her. At first, I couldn't handle the price of popularity, the loss of privacy. It took a while to get used to it, and to learn to deal with it. These days, Trisha and I are best friends, we talk all the time.

"Having so many siblings has helped build my confidence. Even now, when things get hard and I think — what do I have? There's something very real: my family. And because of them, I'll always have close friends. Those are the people who'll always be there for me. For the first time, I feel like my life is almost perfect."

USHER

When a reporter from the music industry bible, *Billboard*, interviewed Usher Raymond about his hit second CD, *My Way*, the twenty-year-old singer explained that if you listen to the songs, "You can definitely pick up on who I am as a person and what I've gone through. I just took things from my life and wrote about them. It's my vision, which is why I named the album *My Way*."

Usher's way wasn't always easy. A native of Chattanooga, Tennessee, Usher and his fourteen-year-old brother, James, were raised by a single parent — their mother, Jonnetta Patton. In a *Vibe* magazine article, Usher's mother, who is also his manager, explained that her son's father "has never been a part of his life."

The absence of his father was something Usher had to accept as he was growing up. But he never had time to feel sorry for himself — mainly *because* of his mother. In a cover story in *Interview* magazine, Usher credited his mom with making his childhood safe and happy. "Me and my mother have a very open relationship. But these last few years, my mother has allowed me to make decisions for myself — to become a man. But she's gonna watch my back — as my mother, as my manager, as my best friend — seeing as how I never had a father. She showed me the difference between good and evil. My dad never did. He split when I was born."

Jonnetta supported her sons both emotionally and financially. She worked very hard. And she tried very hard to keep her sons out of trouble. For Usher, it was to have him start singing in their church choir. Actually, Jonnetta was the choir director at St. Elmo Missionary Baptist Church in Chattanooga, and Usher was singing with her when he was nine years old. Even then it was obvious that he had a special talent.

In the next four years many things changed for Usher. His mother moved her little family to Atlanta, Georgia, and Usher started appearing in talent shows. When he was thirteen, Usher was discovered by Bryant Reid, the brother of LaFace Records president L. A. Reid. By the time Usher was fourteen, he had a record contract with LaFace. And he had a mentor, L. A. Reid. "It's more or less a father-son type thing with me and L. A.," Usher told *Vibe* magazine. "I've never really had a father, and L. A. is like a father to me in this industry. I call him Pop."

Indeed, Usher is very open about how he dealt with growing up without a father. In a candid conversation, Usher recalled his childhood. He knows there are many, many kids who are going through the same things he did, and he hopes his story will give them inspiration.

"I never noticed my father was missing."

"My mother has always been in the struggle, being a single parent and raising two boys. Actually I never noticed my father was missing. I never noticed that I *should* have a father. My mother always made it fun for me. We were always a team.

"As far as guidance, I found it being involved in the church. I found a guy who was like a father, and that's who I would talk to if I needed help or something. The church gave me a lot of balance and understanding of life. I noticed how my mother led her life. She was spiritually grounded — she believed and trusted [in God]. Even though you can't see [Him], you have to believe. It starts with trust. You have to put your trust in [Him], and things start opening up. And since the beginning, I've had nothing but a great life. Sure, times have been hard, but that only made it easier in the long run. Now, I can advise my brother. It taught me to be a team. When you have a smaller team, you have a stronger team. A tighter team. Really."

Usher says he never spent time asking why his father wasn't in his life. He never blamed himself for his father leaving, as so many kids from broken homes do. Those who loved him kept Usher positive. When things came up and Usher needed to have a man-to-man talk or someone to set a good male example, he looked to his close circle of family and friends.

"I would take bits and pieces from life. I would see my cousin's parents or my friends' fathers. I wouldn't let them know I needed a father or that I was looking for a father. I would just take bits and pieces. And I would talk to my mother. [Except] about sex and stuff like that! I *could* go to my mother, but I decided to go to my cousin, Rico. It was like, 'Yo, man, I don't understand these feelings.' He was about eighteen then, and he kept me up with what was going on."

"When it's time for me to be a father, I'll be there for my child."

Usher and his mom were — and still are — very open about their family situation. And there have been times when there was a possibility that Usher's father might have reentered his life. Jonnetta was always honest with Usher. She never made him feel he had to choose between her and his father. It was always up to Usher to do what he wanted.

"She always said it was my own decision [to see my father]. At times he may have tried to come back into my life . . . like when I was around fourteen. My mother was like, 'If you want to talk to your father, it's okay. If you want to let him in your life, go ahead.'

"But was he ever there for me? Was he there for me when I needed diapers or milk or formula? Nope. Was he there when I took my first step? Nope. Did he hear my first word? Nope. But I never missed it. . . . Like I said, my father was never needed. But one thing it taught me: When it's time for me to be a father, *I'll* be there for my child. I'll know what it is to be a father. I'll just do the opposite of what [my father] did."

Unfortunately there are many kids who are growing up in single-parent families but don't have the solid base Usher had. But the super-successful singer says there are definite steps you can take. It's all about parents and children being open and honest with each other. And it's about believing in your own self-worth. He hopes that his success will encourage kids his age to do something with their lives. "They can do it. Look at me — look at what happened!" Usher says encouragingly, and then offers the following advice.

"Wherever I go, I leave with this quote: 'Strivers achieve what dreamers believe.' You can apply that to this [situation]. If a kid is looking for a father or a mother figure, I advise the parent who is there to get involved in their children's lives. They are yours. They didn't have to be born — you brought them into this world. It's your responsibility. Don't let your kids be raised by TV or school. You raise your child to be who you want him or her to be. If you want them to be respectful, you've got to teach them to be respectful. You have to teach them the difference between right and wrong.

"And, I'd tell the kids to listen to your parents and just know if you keep your head to the sky, God will keep you tight. He'll make sure you don't stray in the wrong direction."

MONICA

"AT ONE POINT IN MY LIFE, I BLAMED MYSELF FOR MY FATHER LEAVING."

For singer Monica, 1998 was a killer year. The now eighteen-year-old released her second album, *The Boy Is Mine*, and watched it go multiplatinum. The first single, also called "The Boy Is Mine," was a duet with the other one-named teen singing phenom, Brandy, and it rode the number one spot on the music charts for two months. The reviews for the single, as well as for the entire album, were brilliant. A *Newsweek* magazine writer wrote, "In the world of R&B, people know Monica as a seventeen-year-old Atlanta-born singer with a voice as big as Aretha [Franklin]'s and street smarts to match. . . . Monica establishes herself as the heir apparent to such divas as Whitney Houston and Anita Baker."

Monica and Brandy teamed up on "The Boy Is Mine" for a couple of reasons. First, it was a perfect vehicle for both of them. But more important, the two wanted to put to rest industrywide gossip: That the two singers, who both had burst onto the music scene in 1995, hated each other.

The professional recognition of a hit song was important to Monica, but she was also especially glad to shred the nasty rumor about her and Brandy. Monica knows firsthand how destructive negative feelings can be for your outlook on life. You see, settling miscommunications was a vital part of 1998 for Monica. It was also the year when she finally reestablished a relationship with her long-absent father, M. C. Arnold, Jr.

Finding a father figure

When Monica was four years old, her parents split up. Her mother, Marilyn, worked as a Delta Air Lines customer service representative to support her children, Monica and little brother Montez. They lived right outside of Atlanta in College Park, Georgia. From the very beginning, Monica was very close to her mother. As a two-year-old, Monica would accompany Marilyn when she went to sing in the church choir. Obviously, Monica picked up a thing or two and was soon exercising her own vocal cords. "She was always singing," Marilyn told *People* magazine. "She would have a pencil or a flashlight — anything — using it as a pretend microphone, and just sing her little heart out."

Even when she was a child, Monica's voice seemed to touch hearts. Her early gospel influence added a husky, soulful quality to Monica's sound. And by the time she was eleven and singing in local talent shows, people had to stop, look, and listen when they heard this mature, sophisticated sound coming from such a little girl.

One of those who *really* listened was super-producer Dallas Austin. He was introduced to Monica by a talent scout who had checked her out at a local competition. There was an instant connection between the two, and Monica told *People* magazine, "When we met, it was like I was born all over again. He was the one strong male figure [who] never let me down."

In 1995 Monica released her first Dallas Austin–produced album, *Miss Thang*. It went double platinum — not bad for a fourteen-year-old! The whirlwind of TV and radio appearances, promotional tours, and just being on the road for weeks at a time was exciting for Monica. But it was also hard. There were times Monica was homesick; after all, there was a lot going on back in Atlanta. Her mom had married Rev. Dr. E. J. Best, Jr., in 1993, and soon the family was expanding. Monica missed her brother Montez, and she wanted to get to know her two new baby brothers.

There definitely was a lot of love to go around. But even though Monica now had two father figures in her life — Rev. Best and Dallas Austin — she began thinking about her own dad. It was time to make a move, but it wasn't easy. Monica had been very hurt when her father left years before, and it had taken her a while to really sort out and understand her feelings.

It is these feelings and this journey to understanding, acceptance, and eventual forgiveness that Monica shares. Maybe you can relate to her story; maybe you can learn from it.

"She made a way out of no way."

"I lived in a single-parent home. Of course, we didn't have a lot of money, but my mother kept us comfortable. Mentally I was stable for someone my age, because my brother and I had a lot of responsibility. Montez is three years younger.

"My mother always took care of home, and we never really lacked in a lot of areas. It built me emotionally and physically, and, of course, it built me professionally because it prepared me for a lot of situations. . . . But no matter if [my mother] was at work or right around the corner or sitting right next to me, I never forgot that she was *always* there. She always found a way to make sure my brother and I were comfortable. I never felt like she didn't spend enough time with us. Any time off was time for us. We spent weekends together, we went to church together, even without much money she allowed for vacations to places like Hawaii. This was way before my career. So she made a way out of no way."

But even the love of her mother couldn't stop a certain ache in Monica's heart. She was just a little girl when her father left the family, and she didn't understand. As she got a little older, Monica was even more confused by the situation, and she started acting out her pain.

"Sometimes it got really violent."

"At one point in my life, Montez and I didn't get along. . . . I didn't know why my father was no longer with us. . . . I was used to having him there until I was five or so. [When he left], it didn't make sense to me — I didn't get it. It's traumatic to lose someone you love. . . . I blamed myself and my brother for that. I would be extremely mean to my brother. I was really mean to him until I reached the age of ten. Sometimes it got really violent. I threw him into a television set at one point. That's when I woke up."

Perhaps it was that brother-sister fight that shocked Monica into understanding her internal battle. Whatever it was, things began to change. Monica fully understood that she had to deal with life as it was, not as she wished it would be.

"I realized I was growing up faster than my father. He still had a teenage [boy's] mentality. But it helped me to grow up, and I began to have love for my brother — it was a bond with my brother. It was almost like I was going to father us. . . . Actually, we both made a lot of efforts as far as each other was concerned. Today Montez is my right hand. If something was to ever come about in my life, I would definitely say he's one of the few people I could share those things with."

Since that time, things have definitely been all good for Monica and her family. She's become a number one recording artist. She's even considering taking the next step into films. And there's one more thing — Monica and Montez's dad is back in their lives. Montez spends weekends with his dad, and Monica admits that she's learned to forgive. Of her dad now, she says, "He's matured as a man and a father."

And now, free of all those blinding emotions of her youth, Monica can grow and develop into the woman she was always meant to be.

WILSON CRUZ

"IT HURTS TO FEEL THAT WHO YOU ARE . . . ISN'T ENOUGH FOR YOUR FAMILY."

Fans of TV's legendary *My So-Called Life* won't soon forget Wilson Cruz and his heartrending portrayal of Ricky, a sensitive, loyal, funny, sometimes reckless best friend to Claire Danes's Angela and A. J. Langer's Rayanne. Ricky was TV's first gay teenager. Watching him deal with his complex feelings, with his family's reaction, made for compelling, pioneering, gut-wrenching drama.

Since *MSCL*, Wilson's career has been in high gear. He guest-starred in a memorable episode of *Ally McBeal*; originated the role of Angel in the Los Angeles production of the stage musical *Rent*; and turns up on the big screen in the movies *Supernova* and *Punks*. No matter what career heights he reaches, however, the actor will always be proudest of the work he did on *MSCL*. Being on that show allowed the now openly gay actor to come out publicly. In that way, he was able to reach out and help other young people who desperately needed to hear his voice.

Wilson says, "My goal is to talk about it as much as possible, because not enough people are talking about it. There are so many kids out there who are contemplating suicide, who are committing it. And it breaks my heart. Whatever I can do to talk to these kids, to assure them that things will get better, I will do."

Sharing his own story is one powerful way of doing just that.

"I always knew I was different."

"I was born in Brooklyn, in 1973. I'm the oldest of three kids in a Puerto Rican family. When I was ten, we moved to Michigan because my parents wanted to get us as far from New York City as you can get. Two years later, we moved again, to Riverside, California, and then to Rialto, California, which is where I went to junior high and high school.

"I really can't remember a time when I didn't feel . . . different. I was going to say 'special.' I like that better. I knew there was something weird about me — not even talking sexually. I was always a little different from everyone else at school. I was a little more mature than everyone in my class, even though I was often the youngest in the class. I was always involved in dance, choir, and band, to the exclusion of sports. I was so unacceptable in PE. I was the very last one picked for teams, and every time they chose up sides, I died. It's heartbreaking to think about it. If they had not given us points for actually showing up, I would have failed PE."

The moment I knew: I cried

"I didn't really know why I felt different. But when I was thirteen, I remember watching an afternoon talk show, either *Donahue* or *Oprah*, I can't remember which one. But it was a show with gay people talking about how they felt when they were growing up. I remember watching it going, 'Uh-*huh*. Umm, uh-huh.'

"That was a click, a moment when I could identify with other people's experiences and count them among my own.

"And I remember crying because I knew that — that was *it*.

"And I didn't want to hurt my family, my mom and my dad. And I knew that it definitely would. I knew their attitude about gays because of household conversations. They weren't pointed at me, but just talking about so-and-so and this and that. Back then, the media wasn't as sensitive to the issues, so that when there was something on TV or on the news, derogatory comments were made.

"Later on, my uncle died of AIDS. He wasn't gay. But just the issue being talked about in my home freaked me out. There was a shame and a strong need, by the family, to make it clear to people that he wasn't gay.

"So because of those things and other things that had been said . . . I knew this [telling them] wasn't going to go down well.

"I already thought my dad was ashamed of me. And I'm the oldest son, I carry his name. I felt a responsibility to live up to what he wanted. For my dad, that was always about me being a man, which meant machismo. I was *not* a macho kid. My father would make comments like, Why wasn't I athletic? I should be playing ball, it should be more important to me. But it wasn't.

"Sports held no interest for me whatsoever. I was kinda cocky about it, too. My dad would say, 'Well, why don't you want to do this?' And I'd go, 'Because it's stupid. They're throwing a ball from one side of the field to the other. It makes no sense to me. They're hitting a ball with a bat. Morons can do that.'

"My saving grace as far as my parents were concerned was that I did really well in school academically. They were very proud of that and could brag about it."

The loneliest time of my life

"I couldn't find any books on the subject of homosexuality. I remember going to the small little library in Rialto and looking it up. They didn't have anything. They said to ask at the front desk. And I was like, I am not *about* to go ask at the front desk.

"I felt like there was no place I could go to find out more or anyone I could talk to about how I was feeling. Not at home, not at school, not at church.

"There was one kid, Brian, who was probably the most flamboyant person I'd ever met in my life. I met him in junior high school, and I would avoid him like the plague, because I didn't want to be identified with him. But I liked him — I mean, he was a great guy and he made me laugh.

"High school was rough. While I was dealing with the usual stuff — grades, getting into college, what do I want to do with my life? — I was also trying to figure out how best can I deal with this? How best can I keep my identity from my family?

"I wasn't a loner at school. I had friends, lots of them. It was just weird, because I always felt like I needed to be the person *they* wanted me to be. I was always the funniest person in the class, witty, and always had an answer for everything. I could always help you out with your homework. I was probably the best friend you could possibly have, because I could help you with everything. Other people sought me out; I was pretty popular. I knew everyone, and everyone knew me and came to me — but yet they didn't really know me.

"It was the loneliest time I've ever had in my life, even though I was surrounded by so many people. I longed for a day when I could just climb up on something and just yell what it was that was eating at me.

"Friends are people you're supposed to open up to, but for me, that was not an option. If anything, I avoided that. It became more about, What can I do for you? How can I help you? Don't talk about me — you don't need to know about me.

"And at the same time, it hurt to feel that what I was, and who I was, wasn't enough, for my family and for my friends. And that you had to make excuses to make everybody else happy. And that your happiness wasn't as important to you as much as keeping everyone else happy. Which is a position I would never take again. I will never sacrifice my happiness for someone else again. I'll share my happiness and relish it, but I'll never give it up for anyone again.

"But at the time I didn't know that.

"Among kids in school who weren't my friends, I got teased incessantly. It was always a running joke that I was gay. But I didn't admit it, no. Act offended is what I'd do. There was a lot of acting going on! It's probably why so many great actors are gay — they had years of practice!

"Of course, I *tried* to conform, because I thought that's what I was supposed to do, and that it was a phase. I went through a period where I said [to myself] I was bisexual, because that was, in my mind, more acceptable. It made more sense. That way I could say I was different, yet I could still be the same if I chose. I could walk that line. I do believe that exists, that's possible. But for me it wasn't. It was more of a cop-out than anything else.

"I went out on a date with a girl, once. Poor girl. At the beginning of my senior year when I was still going through my bisexuality stage and I thought, I can do this. But it didn't go well. It was just not right. She knew it wasn't right. I knew it wasn't right. It was awkward; it didn't make any sense; it felt forced, there was nothing natural about it, so it just kinda stopped.

"Finally, in my junior year, I decided to make friends with Brian. I said, Forget it, this is a great kid, I don't care what anybody thinks. He was the first person I met who just didn't care what anybody thought, and I felt there was power in that. And I respected him for that. And I wanted to feel like that, like I just didn't care what anybody thought. Of course, he could hide less than I could. He was just naturally flamboyant. He didn't have much of a choice — whereas I did."

The worst time: It would be better if I weren't here

"The worst time was when I felt . . . it would be better if I weren't here. When I just didn't want to [live], when getting out seemed better than staying. And that just stems from hopelessness. When you don't see or feel that it's going to get any better. Ever. When it's always going to be a big lie. When I contemplated suicide, seriously, I was fifteen or sixteen. I just had no hope. I had no clue that I could do better, that it would be better, that I would have a great life. And I think that's why most people do it.

"What stopped me from committing suicide was my mom. She had lost her brother, and his death was so hard on her and on my family, and I just couldn't do that to her. I couldn't be responsible for her pain again, in that way. So I just couldn't do it."

A support group: Helping one another

"One turning point for me was my senior year. I don't even know exactly how it all came together, but I formed a support group. There were, like, five of us who were out to each other. Brian and I were friends, and Brian and John were friends, and it went from there. We were a multiracial group, Puerto Rican, black, Palestinian, Vietnamese. We just helped each other out, through it. We'd hang out, talk to each other about our feelings, what we were dealing with, helped each other through this horrible time. And that was amazing. Finally, there were people I could talk to, who I could open up to, who could talk to me, people who felt similar things and had gone through similar things [at home]. It was a huge relief. And they're still friends of mine today."

"I answered [my dad] truthfully. And he asked me to leave."

"I still hadn't told my family. And I didn't until I'd begun acting professionally and had won the role of Ricky in *My So-Called Life*. I was nineteen. I came out to my mom first. She took it hard, but she came around very quickly. She cried for about a day, and then

it was all cool. We agreed that we weren't going to tell my father —
not anytime soon, anyway.

"But I knew that I was going to be playing this character on national TV and with it, being interviewed on TV, in magazines, and
newspapers. And I also knew that I was going to be honest about
who I was. It was just something I wanted to do for myself and for
anyone else who was going through what I had.

"So I knew that I had to come out to my dad, because I wouldn't
let him find it out in a newspaper. I thought I would do it just before I left for Los Angeles to start the show, but that didn't happen.
What happened is, Christmas Eve, that year, my whole extended
family was at my house for a huge party. When I was alone with my
father, he just asked me, point-blank, if I was gay. And I said,
'Yeah.' I answered him truthfully.

"And he asked me to leave.

"And so I did. I got in my car. One of my friends was with me,
and he gave me money. I didn't know where I was going. I drove to
L.A., 'cause I didn't know where else to go. I lived in my car until
we started the series.

"My father's reaction didn't exactly surprise me. I knew it was either going to be that or it was going to be violent. I'm glad it was
the one that it was.

"It was hard on my mom — not that we talked about it. She was
angry at him. She didn't side with him. I could have come back
home at one point a month later, but I didn't want to because I was
angry at his response. And I would have rather been on my own
and fended for myself than to deal with him at that point. So she
was just in pain a lot. And I called her, let her know I was okay and
alive and not to worry. But that was probably the hardest point in
my life so far. Because you just don't know what to do, and you

don't have any money. All the horrible stuff I anticipated came to fruition. Although my dad has come a long way — talk about a journey! — and he now accepts me and is proud of me, back then it was rough."

I wanted to be a beacon for kids

"When I started *My So-Called Life*, the activist in me came out. I wanted my character, Ricky, to be a light for kids. I wanted him to be a beacon for anyone who didn't fit in — or felt they didn't fit in — and say it's OK. I'm so proud of that show, I miss it. I was angry when it was canceled. But I look back on it and say, that was enough. Ricky made it from the confusion of the first episode to the last episode when he says, yes, I'm gay. And that's a huge journey. And we did it in a very believable, responsible way. I'm so proud of it."

When you come through the pain, you will be whole and free

"There's no one thing I can say that will make sense for every person who went through what I did. All I can say is, from my own personal experience, if you're true to yourself and who you are, then in the end, you will be satisfied with who you become. And that it's easier now. The pain is always, but all pain is temporary. And when you come through it, you will be whole and free. And when you come to that place of freedom, you will be able and capable of great things — of inspiring, of creating, of living the life that you were put here to live.

"And this: *What* you feel and *how* you love is not as important as that you *do* feel and that you *do* love. If you can hear that at the age of twelve and thirteen and get through the next five or six years, maybe they won't suck. Because if I'd have known then what I know now, I would have felt, OK, I'm going to get through this, because it's going to get better.

"I like to think times are changing. Granted, there are people who don't understand and probably never will, and that's fine. That's what diversity is about.

"But just the fact that we can talk about it out loud and that so many people have come out publicly and shared their stories makes it easier. It would have made it a hell of a lot easier for me.

"I think that's why I'm here."

LeAnn Rimes

Although LeAnn doesn't like to talk about her parents' 1997 divorce, she did admit in Entertainment Weekly, "It was hell on me. I'd known [about their troubles] for a long time. They've always lived for me more than for their relationship, I think. And they stayed together for me." [US]

Harvey Silver (One World)

"My mom put me up for adoption when I was a baby. I was never placed in a private family, I was placed in a lot of group homes. I was easily in twelve–fifteen homes altogether. I would stay until I wanted to move. I didn't want to be tied down. It's a miracle how I came out. [Many] kids turn to drugs. You have no support whatsoever. I made 'quick' friends until I moved on to the next place. I used to be real quiet, especially moving around so much. I felt out of place. I couldn't even ask for food, because I was scared. I had a very deep voice when I was little and I was scared to talk. I thought people would think I was weird. I mean, I was already insecure about not having parents.

"When I was fourteen, I saw a movie with Denzel Washington, and I said, 'Hey that's something I want to grow into. Not the acting at first, just him as a person. I liked that he was smart and educated, but he was cool and hip at the same time. I thought I wanted to be someone like that. So I started doing plays. I went to a community playhouse and started taking drama classes in high school. A friend of mine had a manager who represented Seth Green, Chris Young, and a few other actors. We met and I started going on auditions.

"To any kid out there who's going through what I did? The proof is in the pudding. Look at me talking now. At one point, people thought I was crazy to come out to L.A. to act, since I came from foster care. So don't give up. [Determination] will take you places, like it took me. Whatever you want to do, I would say, stay focused and stay with your dreams, whatever they are."

Kate Winslet (*Titanic*)

The *Titanic* star is from a family of actors — grandparents, father, and siblings. That she has become the most successful has become a bit of an issue. In the *London Daily Mail* it was revealed that Kate's mother said, "We are all utterly sick of all the attention Kate's career has brought. It's not as if she's the only one in the trade. Kate's success makes life difficult for all of us."

Kate has acknowledged the difficulty. In *Rolling Stone,* she conceded guilt feelings. "[My older sister] Anna was going to be the actress. And suddenly little sister comes running along and speeding ahead. It does make me feel bad." Kate has tried to share the wealth of opportunity, by attempting to snare acting roles for her clan in some of her projects — she's been only minimally successful so far. "I hope this year to be able to buy them a house, see them set up properly. I'll be happy then. I'll feel like I've really done it."

Will Friedle (*Boy Meets World*)

"I'm five years younger than my brother Greg and eight years younger than Gary. I looked up to them like you wouldn't believe. They were really responsible for my well-being. Unfortunately, they didn't always get the 'well' part of well-being. Once, when I was four and Greg was nine, we were playing hide-and-seek. I'm sure Greg didn't mean to hurt me when he suggested I hide in the clothes dryer. It was one of those automatic tumble dryers where if you shut the door, it turns on. I got in and the next thing I know I'm going around and around. Luckily, I was only in there for a few seconds when my mother came running down!

"When I was sixteen or seventeen, they really started teasing me. I had started acting and they warned me not to get a big head. So one day I was sitting with my family and my girlfriend was there. I said something that Greg and Gary thought egotistical — I don't even remember what. They grabbed me and took me into the bathroom, dunked my head in the toilet, and flushed. Right in front of my girlfriend! But, as I got older, we developed more of a relationship, we're good friends now. I would call my brothers if I need advice for anything. I guess the teasing stops with time and maturity. Then you become real friends."

LEONARDO DiCAPRIO

5

TYRONE BURTON

BRIAN LITTRELL

Mark Wahlberg

MONEY, SCHOOL AND HEALTH ISSUES

SCOTT ROBINSON

JIM CARREY

BENJAMIN SALISBURY

Matt Damon

JOSHUA JACKSON

TOM HUNTINGTON

James Van Der Beek

ROB THOMAS

Money. There may be more sayings about money than there are about love, from "the love of money is the root of all evil" to "money is power." It divides the "haves" from the "have-nots." Whatever. Maybe Puff Daddy had it right: "It's all about the Benjamins." And if you don't have enough, it's serious i$$ue time. Most of today's top stars are well compensated for their work — but they weren't always so well off. See how they coped.

School. Doing classroom time is one thing that unites us. Some people sailed through those "K-12" years unscathed; for others, the scars still haven't healed. Whether it's GPA meltdown, social stigma, or teachers who tormented, issues abound. You might be surprised at which celebs were totally not cool with school, and how they got through it.

Health. Most people take good health for granted — it's only when we're sick that it becomes an issue. Luckily, most illnesses are short-lived. But when they're chronic, painful, or make us unable to do everyday things, they can color every other aspect of our lives. Think all your favorite stars have dodged the health bullet? Think again — and read on.

LEONARDO DiCAPRIO

"I LIVED IN THE GHETTOS OF HOLLYWOOD. . . . IT WAS THE MOST DISGUSTING PLACE TO BE."

Leonardo DiCaprio, the twenty-four-year-old actor who declared himself "king of the world" in *Titanic*, has definitely come a long way from his early Hollywood days. Yes, Leonardo is from Hollywood, but not from the beautiful communities like Beverly Hills or Bel Air. He grew up in Echo Park, a lower-middle-class Hollywood neighborhood where most families struggled to keep a roof over their heads and food on the table. "When I grew up, I lived in the ghettos of Hollywood," Leonardo told *Movieline*. "Right near the old Hollywood Billiards. It was the crack and prostitution crossroads of L.A. My mom came to this country from Germany when she was very young. She met my dad in college. They moved out to L.A. because they heard it was such a great place, and then my mom became pregnant. They moved right into the heart of Hollywood because they figured that's where all the great stuff was going on in this great town. Meanwhile, it was the most disgusting place to be."

To *Premiere* magazine, Leo described his childhood years similarly. "We were in the poorhouse," he said. "I would walk to my playground and see, like, a guy open up his trench coat with a thousand syringes. . . . To this day it's an imprint on my mind."

However, behind the DiCaprio front door — actually front *doors*, since Leo's parents, Irmelin and George, separated when he was a year old — things were very different. Leo was close to both his parents, even though they weren't together. Irmelin, who then was a legal secretary, and George, who produced and distributed underground comic books, remained friendly.

"Leonardo got a very alternative look at things early on."

If Leo's childhood wasn't luxurious, it was interesting. His mom told *People*, "When I was pregnant, George and I were in a museum looking at a painting by [Leonardo] da Vinci. The baby started kicking — we thought it was a sign." The culture-loving side of Leo comes from Irmelin. "She's always instilling European values in me, things about health, relaxation, exercise, and food," Leo told *YM*.

Leo got his wild side from his dad. George DiCaprio has described himself as a "longhaired, old hippie," and Leo remembers his father's house being the center of all sorts of creative and weird types. Author William Burroughs and poet Allen Ginsberg, legends of the Beatnik era, had George arrange readings for them. Underground comic book creators R. Crumb and Harvey Pekar were often guests at George DiCaprio's house. One of Leo's closest childhood friends was America Hoffman, the son of 1960s antiwar activist Abbie Hoffman. "Leonardo got a very alternative look at things early on," says George.

Of course, Irmelin enjoyed those carefree days, too, and Leo says he would be hard-pressed to do something that would shock his parents. "Whatever [wild thing] I did would [be] something they'd already done," Leo mused on *Scotland on Sunday*. "I mean, my dad would welcome it if I got a nose ring."

Looking back on those days, Leo appreciates the values his parents instilled in him. "My parents were so good at keeping my environment strong and keeping everything around me *not* focused on the fact that we were poor," he told *Interview*. "They got me culture. They took me to museums. They showed art to me. They read to me."

Even though Leonardo's childhood was unconventional, he grew up with a warm and loving extended family. His stepbrother, Adam Farrar, is only three years older than Leo, and they had a close relationship. Both loved to entertain, and when Leo was five years old, he landed his first TV job. "My mom got me on *Romper Room* — it was my favorite show," Leo told *Interview*. "But they couldn't control me. I would run up and smack the camera, and I'd jump around and do my little flips and routines. I wish I could get that tape now."

"Leonardo Retardo"

It wasn't long before he got fired from *Romper Room* for being disruptive. A few years after that, Adam started doing TV commercials, and Leonardo followed suit. His first commercial was for Matchbox cars, and he began appearing in a number of other commercials. By the time Leo was fourteen, the acting roles started coming back to back. First there was TV — sitcoms *Growing Pains* and *Parenthood*. Next came Leo's first feature film, *This Boy's Life*, in which he costarred with Robert De Niro and Ellen Barkin. Pretty heady company for a first movie! The funny thing is that Leo's Marshall High classmates hardly saw him as a would-be teen idol or talented actor. Believe it or not, today's romantic big-screen sigh-guy was once teased by his classmates and nicknamed "Leonardo Retardo."

"He was skinny, kind of wimpy-looking," former classmate Susanna Mejia told *Teen People*. "The girls didn't think he was a babe, not like now."

However, Leo's ninth-grade drama teacher, Helen Stringos-Arias, told *People* that there was something special about him when he went into character. "You just couldn't help but gravitate toward what he did. When he did his monologue, it was so moving that he had the class in tears."

What Leo's ninth-grade teacher recognized in him would soon be one of the most sought-after qualities in Hollywood. Those who worked with Leo, even early on, saw it, too. Alan Thicke, star of *Growing Pains*, discussed Leo's screen magic with *People* magazine, "We had the sense then that nothing was ever going to stop him. He just lit up the place."

Thicke was absolutely correct. After *This Boy's Life*, Leo went on to star in the films *What's Eating Gilbert Grape, The Basketball Diaries, Total Eclipse, William Shakespeare's Romeo + Juliet, Marvin's Room, Titanic,* and *The Man in the Iron Mask*. He was then signed on to be in Woody Allen's *Celebrity* and *The Beach*.

"I'd be miserable in a mansion, all by myself."

In 1998, after *Titanic*, Leonardo joined Hollywood's elite movie stars. It's called the twenty-million-dollar club, which means, along with actors such as Jim Carrey, Tom Cruise, Bruce Willis, and Arnold Schwarzenegger, Leonardo DiCaprio will get the top level salary for his next big budget movie. So what does a twenty-four-year-old who did not grow up in the lap of luxury do with twenty million dollars? Well, one choice might be to go on a spending spree — cars, real estate, clothes, jewelry, and parties. Not Leo. It was only in November 1997 that Leo moved out of his mom's three-bedroom home in Los Feliz, California, for his own place in L.A. — and Leo rents it! The one expense Leo is known for is flying his buddies to the sets of his movies so they can hang out together. But once the guys get to their destination, it's more like a frat pack than a brat pack. Usually everyone stays together, whether it's a roomy house in South Beach, Florida, or a two-bedroom apartment in Paris.

Most of the time, Leo doesn't even carry money with him. It doesn't impress him. He thinks the big bucks flash of Hollywood is simply silly. "The money they throw around doesn't get me," he told *The New York Times*. "What would I need all that money for anyway? I'd be miserable in a mansion, all by myself. I don't want to sound like I'm some underprivileged kid, but you learn certain values. Like not accepting that because you're in a hotel you have to pay five dollars for a Coke — just go down the block for a three-dollar six-pack!"

Leo has credited his parents with his down-to-earth outlook on life. Because of their example, Leo is not overwhelmed by his success, either the fame or the fortune. Irmelin and George, who today are Leo's managers, gave him a childhood he would never trade. "My parents are so a part of my life that they're like my legs or something," the young actor told *Vanity Fair*. "And it wasn't like they created a false good time — that they went out of their way to show me the fabulous things. It was just that they were around and they were great."

They also gave Leo a personal foundation to make life decisions. "I grew up in a pretty tough neighborhood," Leo explained to a *Teen* reporter. "That was the tough part of my life. I just had to stay tough myself and develop a plan for doing something better with my life than what the kids were doing around me. I didn't want to waste my life."

BRIAN LITTRELL

Today, twenty-three-year-old Brian Littrell travels all over the world with the Backstreet Boys. He's always on the go, pushing himself to the max. He has more energy than a roomful of playful puppies. There was a time in Brian's life, however, when he could barely lift his head from a pillow, a time when he was literally near death.

The fateful day that almost denied a future to Brian was in 1980. He was five years old and was playing outdoors with his eight-year-old brother, Harold, Jr. They were just fooling around when Brian slipped and fell on a concrete walkway. There was a loud thud as little Brian's skull cracked on the hard surface. Alerted by the wails of their little one, Brian's parents, Jackie and Harold Littrell, scooped him up and rushed him to Good Samaritan Hospital. Though he hadn't knocked himself unconscious, it looked serious.

It was more serious than they ever could have guessed — but it wasn't the gash in Brian's head that nearly killed him. It was a blood infection, a staph infection. "Bacterial endocarditis," Brian told a magazine. "That was the infection, but don't ask me to spell it!"

The Littrells never gave up hope

This infection with the long name threatened Brian's life, so much so that he admits, "I had no chance of living whatsoever. The doctors were telling my parents to go ahead and make funeral arrangements."

Brian's heart had stopped for thirty seconds at one point. The Littrell family held a twenty-four-hour-a-day vigil at the hospital. The doctors were predicting the worst.

The infection was bad enough. But then the doctors discovered Brian's heart problem. The little boy had a tiny hole in his heart. That can sound worse than it is. In fact, the condition is not all that unusual in kids, and often the hole closes by itself as the child grows. For that reason, doctors usually don't operate until it becomes necessary. In Brian's case, the infection had worsened his heart condition. If Brian did pull through, the doctors explained to the Littrells that he would probably be brain-dead. But Harold, Jackie, and Brian's siblings never gave up hope. They prayed; they insisted the doctors try anything and everything. At one point, Brian recalls the doctors actually beating on his chest trying to break up the infection. The five-year-old Brian was in tears . . . but it got worse.

Brian was barely conscious as the doctors and nurses did their best. "I remember them taking me out of bed and putting me in a tub of ice to cool my body off," Brian told *Teen People*. "Then they put me back in bed with only a sheet to cover me. Ten minutes later, they put me back in the ice. This kept up for an hour. Then I blacked out."

Jackie never left Brian's side, and when her little boy opened his eyes and recognized her, she knew the crisis was finally over. "I just had a faith inside that this wasn't the end for Brian," she told *Teen People*. "God just reached down and touched that child, and he started on his way up."

Meet the Backstreet Boys

And though he still had a small hole in his heart, Brian thrived. He was never held back from any activity, except for getting on his high school basketball team because he was too short! But Brian got over the disappointment, because around the same time he had found something he really loved: entertaining. Brian had belonged to his church choir for years, so everyone knew he could sing. But it was in his junior year, when he didn't make the basketball team again, that Brian had a major realization. That very day he went home and told his mom, "I learned something today. I can play ball as good as any of those guys, but none of them can sing like me."

A year later, Brian joined his cousin Kevin Richardson, plus Howie Dorough, A. J. McLean, and Nick Carter to form the Backstreet Boys. Based in Orlando, Florida, BSB actually had to prove themselves first in Europe, Canada, Asia, and Australia before they made it in the United States. But it was worth the wait. Finally, in 1997, the Backstreet Boys were breaking records in their home country. Their debut American album racked up four back-to-back top five hit singles: "Quit Playing Games (With My Heart)," "As Long As You Love Me," "Everybody (Backstreet's Back)," and "I'll Never Break Your Heart." The boys were eagerly looking forward to their first major American tour. Everything they had dreamed about was happening.

Heartbreak

Then Brian found out that he had a heart problem once again. Since his childhood brush with death, Brian always had regular checkups to monitor the condition of his heart. For years everything was fine, but in the spring of 1997 Brian's doctors found his heart was very enlarged and leaking blood. They decided that the congenital hole in his heart had caused the problem. It wasn't life-threatening right then, but could be later on. So in the fall of 1997 it was recommended that Brian undergo heart surgery. But the Backstreet Boys were working nonstop. They had concert dates and promotional appearances in Europe, the United States, and Canada, plus several videos to shoot. Working closely with his doctors, Brian agreed to take a break in the late spring of 1998 to undergo open-heart surgery. If everything went as planned, Brian would be able to have his surgery in May, rest up the entire month of June, and rejoin the Backstreet Boys for the beginning of their summer tour in July.

When word got out that Brian was going to have open-heart surgery, the Backstreet Boys' fans rallied around. They all wanted to send their best wishes to Brian and find out what they could do to make him feel better. Brian responded to the massive queries by setting up a special fund for children with heart problems.

Through the Backstreet Boys' fan clubs, their official website, as well as ads in music industry publications and radio stations, Brian asked his fans, instead of sending flowers, gifts, and cards, to make donations to the Brian Littrell Fund for Pediatric Cardiology at St. Joseph's Hospital in Lexington, Kentucky. The fans responded wholeheartedly!

And Brian really appreciated their good wishes. When *Teen* magazine talked to Brian shortly before he rejoined the Backstreet Boys, he made a point of thanking his fans. "I'm recovering very well, actually, due to the great doctors and a lot of support and love from my family and friends, not to mention all the fans and people sending get well cards," he said. "I'm taking a lot of walks and getting a lot of extra care."

"I didn't know how to approach her."

Since Brian knows what it's like to have health problems, he is very sensitive to fans who are disabled or ill. He knows how lonely it can be in a hospital or confined at home. That's why Brian goes out of his way to reach out to kids who are facing health problems. Shortly before Brian went into the hospital, the Backstreet Boys performed in Orlando, Florida. A. J.'s mom brought a little girl backstage. She was in a wheelchair, and Brian found out she was suffering from two forms of cancer. "I didn't know how to approach her," he told *Spin* magazine. He wanted to let her know that she wasn't alone, that he understood what it was like to be ill. And he wanted to let her know how much he appreciated her support of the Backstreet Boys, even when she was fighting for her life.

"I wanted to say, 'Listen, I'm getting ready to have an operation, too,'" Brian continued telling *Spin*. "So I went over to her mother and told her that, and her mother said, 'Oh, my daughter could tell you a lot of things.' Can you imagine?"

That response only reinforced Brian's belief that part of healing yourself is to reach out to others who might need help. According to Brian, it's just part of the circle of life.

JOSHUA JACKSON

"NO MATTER WHO YOU ARE, THE FIRST YEAR OF HIGH SCHOOL SUCKS. IT'S ALWAYS AN UNCOMFORTABLE TIME."

A cting since he was nine years old, Josh Jackson was probably best known for his role of ice-hockey hero Charlie Conway in all three *Mighty Duck* movies — until, that is, he landed the role of Pacey on *Dawson's Creek*. Those early years as an actor were very exciting for Josh, who is now twenty. He was a natural, and he loved all the attention he received. He didn't even mind moving from his home in Vancouver, British Columbia, Canada, to Los Angeles so he could be available for work. There was one snag in Josh's dream story, though. When he was ten years old, his parents divorced.

"My mother and father breaking up was tough," Josh recalls. "It was really painful because everything you trusted and felt secure about fell apart. After their divorce, I felt anything could happen."

Though Josh maintained a good relationship with his father after the split, the young actor lived with his mom, Fiona, who was a TV and film casting director, and his little sister, Aisleigh (pronounced Ashley). After a while Fiona moved her family back up to

Canada. Josh's life had really changed. "It was just me, my sister, and my mother," he says. "We went at it alone."

"I used to get into so much trouble."

Today, when looking back on those years, Josh admits that he became a handful. There were a lot of pent-up feelings, and he had to release some of that energy building up inside. Acting helped. When he was working, he could live the pretend life of his character and not think too much about the rough hand life had dealt him. Sports was another way to handle his inner emotions. He played basketball, football, baseball, and hockey. Josh excelled on the playing fields. Couple that with his natural charm and fun-loving nature and Josh became very popular with his schoolmates.

However, Josh is the first to admit that his Mr. Popularity claim to fame didn't necessarily trickle over to his teachers. To them, Josh was a handful. His tendency to break up the class with his antics and jokes labeled him class clown to his friends, but troublemaker to the teachers. By the time he entered Vancouver's Kitsilano High School, Josh was dealing with all sorts of demons — his parents' divorce, the pressure of balancing acting and school, and just being a teenager. But at the time, Josh didn't think he was really *so* different from other kids. "No matter who you are, the first year of high school sucks," he says candidly. "It's always an uncomfortable time."

But for Josh, it became *more* than uncomfortable. "I used to get into so much trouble," Josh confesses. "Cracking jokes and talking when I wasn't supposed to. I would get teachers so mad, they would tell me, 'Just get out of the class.'"

Though Josh was often absent from the classroom, either because he was sent to the principal's office or was on a movie location, he still earned decent grades. But that still didn't cut it with some of his teachers. Eventually Josh's behavior had dire consequences.

"At fifteen, I didn't take things seriously," he admits. "And I got kicked out of high school twice — once for attitude and once for lack of attendance. I'd like to say that it was because I was working a lot. But really, I was just a pain in the butt."

"I've never been more ashamed of myself."

When it became obvious that returning to Kitsilano or any other high school was not in the picture, Josh ended up studying on his own, and in 1997 he earned his G.E.D. (General Equivalency Diploma). When a teenager graduates from high school, it's usually time to celebrate. But there was no ceremony for Josh, no marching down the aisle to "Pomp and Circumstance" to pick up his diploma. Instead, getting his G.E.D. was anything but a happy experience. He was embarrassed and angry at himself for taking things so lightly that he couldn't finish high school and graduate with his friends. He felt taking just one test to get his G.E.D. didn't really prove anything, didn't mean he really had accomplished anything. "I've never been more ashamed of myself in my life than when I got to the end of that [G.E.D.] test and just went, 'Oh, God, I can't believe I just did this,'" he says.

It was difficult for Josh to accept that he had wasted those precious years he should have been learning in school. It was something he could never get back. But with the help of those closest to him, Josh was able to learn from his mistake. Of that time, Josh explains, "I went from being a very well-off little kid to having a couple of rough years, to rebuilding — my mother did that. She and I are very close."

Today, Josh still enjoys being a cutup and making people laugh, but he also appreciates exercising his mind. Whether it's on the set of *Dawson's Creek* or his most recent feature films — *Apt Pupil*, *Cruel Intentions*, and *Urban Legend* — you'll usually find Josh's nose buried in a book when he's not in front of the cameras. Somehow it's different now. Josh isn't exploring a subject just to make a grade, he's doing it because he wants to. "I [don't have to be] an A student," he told *Jane* magazine, "but just learning in general is great."

Josh's attitude has changed so much that he told a reporter that acting isn't the *only* dream in his life. He would also like to be an architect. "I'll go to school after the show and figure out what I want to do with the rest of my life," he said.

Now Josh understands the importance of school. "I can read all the books I want, but I can only think with one mind, and I don't have access to a bunch of different people who are tackling the exact same circumstances that I'm tackling, and I just . . . I can't wait. I can't wait to dive in there and do stuff like that."

He's really excited about the future. As for the past, well, Josh knows he can't change that, but one of the reasons he's been so open about his school struggles is he hopes it might help a troubled teenager today. Maybe some fans — even just one — can learn from his mistakes. "Many of the letters I get are from young people," Josh says. "Because of my age and the bond they have with the show, I feel I have an obligation to them. I always try to project a positive influence."

SCOTT ROBINSON

"EVERYONE AT SCHOOL THOUGHT I WAS THICK. AND SO DID I."

Together Scott Robinson, Rich Neville, J. Brown, Abs Breen, and Sean Conlon are known as Five, one of today's hottest British boy bands.

Scott, Rich, J., Abs, and Sean were all into music. In 1997, they each answered an audition ad. Actually, it was a massive cattle call. Three thousand hopefuls from all over the United Kingdom applied. There were competitions at clubs and arenas throughout the country. Eventually the promoters of the auditions narrowed it down to thirteen guys. The end result would hopefully produce two or three boy bands. Of course, the father-and-son team who came up with this idea knew something about putting together a successful group. They were Bob and Chris Herbert, the management team who brought the world the Spice Girls.

Though the Herberts wanted to match up the groups themselves, Scott, Rich, J., Abs, and Sean all seemed drawn to one another. Soon they were off in a corner throwing riffs down. They knew they were a group, and no one could have broken them up from that time on.

Even the Herbert brothers recognized the instant magic of the guys. There was no question — they were a group called Five! Next thing they knew, the lads were living together in a house in Camberley, just outside of London. Needless to say their neighbors will never forget the experience. Just imagine every kind of music from hip hop to pop to grunge rock 'n' roll blasting out the windows of the house all hours of the day. Add five gorgeous guys with their adrenaline pumped to the extreme and you've got the early days of Five.

Even today the guys crack up when they talk about those days. It was fun and it was outrageous, but it gave them the opportunity to fine-tune their act. It also bonded them together, even though each had a completely different background.

Scott's secret

Naturally, on those long, lonely nights on the tour bus or camping out in one motel room between gigs, the guys talked, shared their hopes, dreams, and secrets. Rich and Scott already shared a theater background, so they just sort of started to hang. When Scott confided his biggest secret to Rich, it was the day they knew they could totally trust each other. You see, all through school Scott had been living a lie. A bit hyperactive, Scott seemed more concerned with joking around than studying. Everyone just thought he was funny but dumb. And Scott was too embarrassed to ask for help. Not his classmates, not even his teachers, knew the real story: Scott couldn't read! And he didn't know why. He recalls how difficult it was and candidly shares his feelings back then.

"All the teachers thought I was a troublemaker."

"When I was at normal school, everyone thought I was thick. And so did I. Everyone told me I was dumb, so I'd muck around in a lesson instead of paying attention. I became the class clown, and no one realized what the real problem was. They'd say Scott's getting the laugh because he can't do math and he can't do English. All the teachers thought I was a troublemaker.

"Then, when I left that school, I went to an acting school. I met a new teacher, and she realized the problem. I was dyslexic! She was dyslexic herself. She took me to be tested. I found out that even though I was fifteen, I had the reading level of a seven-year-old.

"I began to tape things. I had a Dictaphone, and I'd tape the classes instead of writing notes. I would speak my homework. I started getting A's for my homework, because I didn't have to write. I know I'm a quite clever person, because I know if I could speak everything, I would have gotten all A's.

"[Because of our busy schedule,] I haven't been reading much. [But] I'm starting to read now. Richard is helping me read now. I'm reading books for younger people. At first I didn't want to do that because I felt stupid. [Sometimes] I still feel stupid reading at a child's level. But I know it's going to help me get better — then, eventually, I can start reading anything I want."

If Scott had not met his teacher and if he had given up and accepted that he was stupid, he wouldn't be in Five right now. But something deep inside Scott kept him going, kept him trying.

"There were some teachers at school who said that I'd never be where I am now," he told *TV Hits* magazine. "There were people who didn't believe [in] me. I don't want to say, 'I told you so' or anything, but those people know who they are, and I'd just like to say to them, 'You were wrong!'"

TYRONE BURTON

"I [SAW] THE OLDER BROTHERS SELLING DRUGS AND MAKING FAST MONEY.... I WANTED WHAT THEY HAD."

Talk about art mirroring life! Tyrone Dorzel Burton is nineteen years old, and during that short time he has traveled from the dangerous streets of Boston's Dorchester neighborhood to every dream opportunity offered by Hollywood, including a role created just for him on the TV series *The Parent 'Hood*. It has been more than a three-thousand-mile trip. It has been much more than a feel-good rags-to-riches story. For Tyrone, it has been a miracle.

Flash back ten years. Tyrone was a little boy headed for big trouble. His family was on public assistance and for a time lived in shelters. Several times, Tyrone's mother had the entire burden of the family, because her husband was in jail. Yet Tyrone had dreams like any other boy. Cars, clothes, money, success. Unfortunately, in Tyrone's world, the only way he saw those dreams coming true was to sell drugs and join a gang.

He was headed down that negative path until two things happened: He was almost killed by a boy he thought was his friend, and he met a youth worker who really cared.

Emmett Folgert was a cofounder of the anti-gang youth center, Dorchester Youth Collaborative (DYC), and he guided Tyrone along a road that has led to super-success. At DYC, Tyrone got involved with a program Emmett had just started: an acting ensemble called Extreme Close-Up (ECU). A natural-born actor, Tyrone quickly landed some commercials and then won a stint as a host on Boston's FOX-Kids TV. As the appeal of the street faded away, Tyrone concentrated on becoming the best actor he could. He took classes and studied with the New African Theater Company. He performed at Boston's Huntington Theater, and for three years he worked on a special project born at DYC. It was the film *Squeeze*. Based on true experiences at DYC, Emmett developed a script about a young African-American teen named Tyson who was nearly destroyed by the violence on the street. Tyrone played Tyson.

Squeeze was the heart of DYC. The main characters of the movie were played by members of ECU. Tyrone's costars were Phuong Van Duong and Eddie Cutanda. A young Boston filmmaker whom Emmett had pulled in to help teach an acting class cowrote the script and directed the film. The project was funded by donations and a few private investors. For three years they lived and breathed *Squeeze* until they had a finished film. That's when the movie company Miramax saw it and decided to distribute it. The film won such critical praise that the Independent Film Project (IFP) nominated it for an Independent Spirit Award in 1998.

Squeeze also introduced Tyrone to Hollywood. After the film was released, he was contacted by producers, agents, and managers. He was sent script after script. But it was actor/director/producer

Robert Townsend who came up with an offer that really intrigued Tyrone. He was asked to read for the role of T. K., a new character on Townsend's WB TV series *The Parent 'Hood*. In early July 1997, Tyrone and Emmett flew out to Los Angeles for the audition. Three weeks later, they were back so Tyrone could start taping the first show of the season.

Today Tyrone is doing what he loves — acting. And he hopes that his personal journey may inspire others. Tyrone has people who inspired him. Emmett Folgert is one, of course. The other is Bill Cosby. "Bill Cosby is such an inspiration in my life, I want to do the same for others. I want to be able to give back and just be a positive role model for others."

Read Tyrone's story — and get inspired.

"The Rude Boys Posse . . . we was da bomb!"

"I was young, about seven years old. We were living on Dakota Street. That was when I was just getting involved with street stuff. You know, I was young. I couldn't stay in the house, so I would go out with my brother and some of my cousins, and we would go out and pump some gas. You know, just for some quarters and whatever. Just to make a little change to have something in our pockets. You know, to get a haircut or to save up and chip in for our school clothes. To add a little to what our mothers would receive from the state.

"We used to go over to the Fill 'Em Fast gas station and pump gas or wipe windshields or over to the Purity Supreme supermarket and help people with their bags and stuff. Sometimes they gave us a quarter, sometimes a dollar, sometimes nothing, but we'd do it for whatever they gave us. At the end of the day we would end up leaving with twenty-three or twenty-five dollars. That would be some money for a kid."

Soon other kids joined the baby entrepreneurs at the gas station, and they started hanging out with one another 24-7. By the time Tyrone was eleven years old, they decided they needed a name. They came up with a perfect tag: Rude Boys Posse.

"Rude Boys Posse — RBP. I swear, we was da bomb! Everyone started to know us. We didn't consider ourselves a gang; we just wanted a name, to be called something to bring us together tighter. We were already friends, but we wanted a name — a name, so we'd own it. Rude Boys started getting a [reputation]. And we started getting involved with things that were going on around the community. There were always abandoned stolen cars on the street. I didn't steal the cars, but I would ride in them. I'd be the one to roll up on ten of my boys, and, like, 'Yo! Wassup, yo, come on, jump on in.' We had this whole lifestyle that became fun to us. We had cars. We started selling drugs. We were making money. We started buying gold, leather jackets. . . ."

"I'm a young kid. Ain't nobody gonna mess with me."

"You know, we would hear about things that happened up the street — someone got shot or something. I felt, 'I'm Tyrone. I'm a young kid. Ain't nobody gonna mess with me.' I really didn't take it serious. You know, other people who haven't grown up in this situation probably would be scared. But we were part of that. We lived that. We probably knew the person who got shot, but we just figured, 'Hey, he got shot. . . .'"

Money lured the Rude Boys Posse into selling drugs. As Tyrone told *Teen People*, "I [saw] the older brothers selling drugs and making fast money, wearing gold. I wanted what they had. I never wanted to kill or hurt anyone — I am not violent. I was attracted to the gold."

It was a dangerous path Tyrone and his friends were taking, but since they were little kids — all of them were between ten and twelve years old — they didn't know just *how* dangerous. To them, selling drugs just meant money to buy things — leather jackets, gold chains, a pair of sneaks. But to the older gangs, the heavy-duty drug dealers, the Rude Boys Posse meant competition. And they weren't going to stand for it. One night, in one terrifying moment, it all came home to Tyrone.

"One time these guys came over to us while we were hanging out. We knew who they were. My brothers and I used to stay overnight at this one guy's house. He put a gun to my head and said, 'Take off your chains.' I took off my chains. I took off my jacket. We were in an isolated hallway. I couldn't go anywhere. He could have killed me right there. That could have been the end of my life. Somehow I got away alive. I thank God that I'm here, that I made it through that experience. I think that's what impacted me the most. It's what made me say, 'Hey, hold on!'"

Even before the gun incident, Tyrone's parents, Darril and Paulette Burton, realized they had to take action. Tyrone was cutting school, heading for big trouble. His mom wanted to find someone or something that could turn him around. That's when the idea of the Dorchester Youth Collaborative came up. DYC had helped many kids stay off the streets. Actually, DYC was the youth center that the musical megastars New Kids on the Block came from. They knew one another from the center, and in the early days they practiced their moves in the back room at DYC.

DYC had also turned things around for Tyrone's cousin Michael. He had started hanging out at the center and hooked up with four other guys to form the rap group Young Nation. They became so popular in the New England area that they were often an opening act at New Kids on the Block concerts. Michael was exposed to a whole new kind of life, and eventually he left the streets behind and went on to college. Tyrone's parents wanted to see if the same could happen for him.

"My mother actually brought me up to DYC, me and my little brother, Darril. I started going to DYC, but I was still bouncing back and forth between there and the streets. When I got the gun held to my head, I told Emmett Folgert, the anti-gang youth worker at DYC. We talked about it. Emmett said: 'Yeah, man, it's getting serious. You gotta make a decision.' He asked us [the Rude Boys Posse] to start coming to DYC."

Emmett knew that to keep Tyrone off the street, he had to find something special to replace it. So Emmett suggested that Tyrone get involved with a program he had just started at DYC, an acting ensemble called Extreme Close-Up. It worked. Acting was just what Tyrone needed.

But there were times that Tyrone and his friends were lured back to the streets. Somehow, Emmett would always show up. Tyrone now laughs about how his youth worker would spy on them. If Emmett asked them if they had been on the street and they said no, they were in the park playing ball, he would pin them right there and then.

"He'd say, 'Yeah, right. I was over there. I rented a car and I was driving through.' He knew what was going on. He'd check us out, and he knew if we were lying or not. Finally he said, 'This is your last chance. You've got to cut it clean or you're out of ECU.'

"That pulled me over to the positive side even more than the gun being pointed to my head. After talking it over with Emmett, I made a decision. I wanted to act. I love acting. Acting is what I like doing. It was like, the streets, my boys, driving stolen cars, making hundreds of dollars a day, all this gear, clothes, girls, radios — I love the streets, I love my boys. But I loved acting more. I realized with acting I can build. I can save money. I can do something I love. I decided to go with acting and I'm never gonna give it up. . . . When you're livin' in the streets you're forced to be closed-minded because you only see the bad stuff, but that [can] make you stronger. You realize life ain't no joke — you've gotta get into something positive and go after what you love to do."

Matt Damon
(Good Will Hunting)

"I was definitely not a fighter when I was a kid. My mother taught non-violent conflict resolution. I did get in one fight at school, and I kept hurting the kid when I should have stopped, and it scared the hell out of me. I still remember the shame. It never left me."
[Details]

James Van Der Beek
(Dawson's Creek)

The star of Dawson's Creek was diagnosed as dyslexic: "They caught it while I was in kindergarten. I learned to read in a special, experimental class."

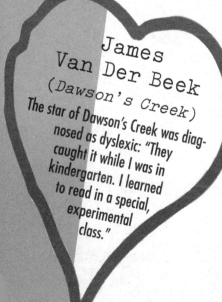

Jim Carrey (The Truman Show)

"When my father, who was an accountant, lost his job he was fifty-one. He couldn't find another job. My family was financially devastated. Suddenly, I was working eight hours in a factory after school. [I was so tired] I went from being the top student in the class to 'I don't understand a word you're saying.' I know how family problems affect teenagers. If it's bad at home, you ain't got an easy deal. There was a bitterness that settled in on us. I used to lie in bed at night and figure out how I would 'fix' the brakes on my father's boss' car. At a certain point, my family threw in the towel and we lived on the road in a van, all around Toronto. It wasn't a real happy time. It's funny, people ask me about the pressures of show business, but nothing compares to the pressure of living in a van. Everything else is a step up." [*Seventeen*]

Tom Huntington
(*Saved By the Bell: The New Class*)

Tom, 21, was born and raised in Wheatland, Missouri, population 363. His mom, Sherry, was a single parent who struggled to support Tom and his younger sister, Chelsea. When Sherry could find a job, it was usually minimum wage and long hours — like when she was a waitress/cashier/gas attendant at Wheatland's filling station/restaurant. But sometimes, there were no jobs at all. During those stretches, Tom's family had to use food stamps. "I feel bad for getting embarrassed, but I just didn't realize that was part of life. Since all the other families didn't use food stamps, that was tough, because everyone knew everyone else. There were times when we didn't have a car, so we'd have to call up friends to take us to the store for groceries. People helped me out with school supplies, because we couldn't afford them. In exchange, I'd mow someone's lawn, or once I had to go to this guy's house in the country and pick rocks out of this old pasture all day."

Tom overcame his embarrassment when he realized no one thought less of his family for needing help occasionally. But those days left a mark. When he left for Los Angeles to become an actor, a huge part of his motivation was to help his family. "Today I still have the dream of getting them a new car and a house."

Benjamin Salisbury (*The Nanny*)

He's been on TV for several years as Brighton on TV's *The Nanny*, but Benjamin Salisbury, now 18, has sharp memories of once being homeless. When his stepdad lost his job, and then deserted the family, five-year-old Ben, his mom, and sisters had no recourse except to live in their car. Benjamin recalls the embarrassment of having to brush his teeth at the 7-Eleven and the fights over who got to sleep lying down and who had to sit up. "We listened to the car radio the way other people watch TV," he told *Teen People*. "And during the day we amused ourselves by playing the windshield wiper game — putting objects on the windshield and sweeping them away with the wipers." The bleak period lasted four months.

Rob Thomas (*Matchbox 20*)

The lead singer of the hot rock group Matchbox 20 grew up in a trailer park in Florida. After getting his GED [general education diploma], he split — and spent the next three months sleeping on a park bench and crashing on friends' couches. Rob is now an advocate for homeless teens, who are mostly runaways. He asks fans to bring old shoes, sleeping bags, and jackets to Matchbox 20 concerts to donate to Children of the Night, and other organizations.

Mark Wahlberg
(actor)

"I definitely grew up in a bad neighborhood and did some bad things. But I think the most rebellious thing I did was break away from the pack and refuse to get into trouble. I wanted something better for myself." [*Jump*]

177

BEVERLEY MITCHELL

DREW BARRYMORE

JEREMY AND JASON LONDON

Prince William and Prince Harry

Dustin Diamond

ISSUES
OF
LOSS

Lauren Holly

TIM ALLEN

SEAN "PUFFY" COMBS

HOWIE DOROUGH

SHANIA TWAIN

Freddie Prinze, Jr.

Live Through This. That was the prophetic title of the group Hole's most famous album. It came out at the same time lead singer Courtney Love had to live through the loss of her husband and soulmate, Kurt Cobain.

The loss of a loved one is by far the worst thing most people ever go through. Does anyone ever get over the death of someone close? Doubtful. The best anyone can do is come to terms with the loss, find peace and comfort, and maybe eventually inspiration in having known the loved one.

There's never a good time to lose a friend or relative. Losing an older adult, like a grandparent, doesn't make it easier. But losing a young person is all the more horrifying, all the worse. Losing someone you love when you're young just isn't supposed to happen. Tragically, it does.

Being a star doesn't shield you from anything, really, least of all life's harshest realities. But the lucky ones learn to cope somehow. Here's how some did.

BEVERLEY MITCHELL

Beverley Mitchell plays Lucy on TV's *7th Heaven*. The show revolves around the Camden family — minister dad Eric, homemaker mom Annie, and their brood, Matt, Lucy, Simon, and Ruthie, plus new baby twins and a dog. While *7th Heaven* is at heart a wholesome family show in which most issues get resolved with wisdom, courage, and a hug, it never shies away from real life and often tackles the tough stuff. Episodes have dealt with such hard-hitting issues as peer pressure, illness, homelessness, drug abuse, and teen parenthood.

One of the show's most powerful and poignant episodes was titled "Nothing Endures But Change." In it, Lucy's friend, a teen driver, is killed in a freak car crash. It made for an hour of gripping TV — shocking, compelling, heartrending, and ultimately cathartic. It received tons of mail from young viewers, many with similar tales to share.

What most viewers didn't know, however, is that Beverley Mitchell herself could relate. For that episode was based on a real life tragedy. This is what happened and how Beverley, now seventeen, was able to find solace and the courage to go on. She shares her story in the hope of letting others who have had to face loss know they're not alone.

(Out of deference to the family of the girl who died and the others involved in the accident, all names have been changed. But the details of the story are true.)

Friends forever — not just for life

"The beginning of middle school is a little scary, because kids from lots of different schools are coming together for the first time, and you're not sure who your friends will be. I was lucky. In homeroom the first day, I met three girls, Lisa, Nicole, and Tammy, and we became instant best friends. We just clicked. From that day on, it was the four of us, we did everything together. We went to the movies, went swimming, did girl things like go shopping, gossip, talk about boys. We went through every day of middle school together and thought we'd be a team all through high school, too.

"Being so tight, of course, we used to get into stupid fights sometimes. I'm the type of person who likes to make everyone feel good, but Tammy was the real peacemaker of the group. She hated when we fought. She'd do her best to make everyone happy, but if that didn't work, she'd get in our faces and go, 'C'*mon*, stop!' And we would, because her smile was like a magnet. She was just a beautiful person, inside and out, kind to everyone. The thing is, she really paid attention to your mood and was sensitive to it. She could be a clown sometimes, but she knew when to get serious.

"I have so many memories of the four of us together. Two stand out. For one of our friend's fifteenth birthday party, a whole group of us went to [the coastal resort town of] Santa Barbara and rented these tandem bikes and six-seater buggies. Since there were a lot of us, we didn't all fit in one buggy. Because I was the smallest, they stuck me in the basket that was attached to it. I have this vivid picture of Tammy pulling up alongside me on her bike and goofing on me. She was always teasing me about being short, but I was catching up to her. Later that day we went Rollerblading and took pictures of ourselves down by the marina eating ice cream, just having fun, being carefree, normal kids.

"The other vivid memory I have is this one time when we made up after a fight. All four of us had been fighting over some stupid stuff. It was, like, 'Well, if *she's* not talking to you, then *I'm* not talking to you — and I don't even know why she's mad at you.' Really dumb stuff like that. But at one point, hurt feelings [had] been building for a while. So one night we all got together and just aired everything out. It was hard, because mean things had been said, and we were all crying. I felt so bad I covered my head with a baby blanket to hide my tears. Suddenly Tammy popped her head under it and started to do all these silly things to make me laugh. It worked, too. Later that night I did the same thing for her. At the end of the night, after it was all over, we had this huge group hug.

"That's the way it was with us. We'd argue, we'd make up. But above all else, we were always there for each other. It was that kind of special friendship, we knew we could count on each other, no matter what. We really thought we'd be together for the rest of our lives. Now we say friends forever. And we take that phrase very seriously. Because forever is longer than the rest of your life."

"Reality's gonna hit right now."

"The day it happened was like any other normal Friday. After school we broke up into a couple of different groups. Tammy and three other girls were driving to a friend's house. Since Tammy was only fifteen, she didn't have her license yet. But she was sitting in the front, next to the driver. Everyone was seat-belted in. No one had been drinking or anything like that. The music wasn't even on too loudly. They had done everything right.

"I was in another car with another friend, and we were headed to her house. As soon as we pulled into her driveway, we knew something was wrong. Her parents were standing in the driveway, waiting for us. That was odd by itself — it was really strange that her dad was home. He never got home that early. And I'll never, ever forget the first words her dad said to us when we got out of the car. 'Reality's gonna hit right now.'

"We tensed, but we had no clue what we were about to hear. Our first reaction, was, 'What did we do wrong?' We couldn't imagine why we would be in trouble, but we couldn't imagine what else he was talking about. Then they told us to come in the house and wait for my parents to get there. Now I was starting to panic. I sat on the edge of the couch, trying to figure out what this was all about. No way in a million years would we have guessed what we were about to hear. Because this — *this* — doesn't happen. We're teenagers. We're good kids.

"Finally my friend's parents couldn't hold out any longer. They said to me, 'Your parents are okay.' That's when it hit me that maybe someone else wasn't. Then they said, 'There's been an accident.'

"My heart stopped. I held my breath. A dozen faces paraded across my mind.

"Finally they told us our close friends had been in a car accident. I was in disbelief. Quietly they said, 'Tammy died.'

"I burst out laughing. I honestly thought it was a joke and started to go, 'Hey, this isn't funny.' But the looks on their faces told me it was no joke.

"It was incomprehensible. It was just a freak car accident — and still no one knows exactly what happened or why. They weren't on a freeway, they weren't speeding, it wasn't dark out, no other cars were involved. But for some reason — maybe the driver swerved — the car just flipped over several times and smashed into a telephone pole. The girl at the wheel was hurt, and the girls in the back were slightly injured. Tammy was the only one killed. She died instantly, her neck broken.

"I was in shock. I couldn't cry. Me, I'm the one who likes to be in control, to make other people feel better. And now I was out of control, I didn't know what to do. My friend and I insisted on going to the hospital immediately, where the other girls were. My parents met us there. It was the weirdest thing I've ever experienced. The two girls who'd been in the backseat were outside the hospital, just stunned. We all went into the emergency room to see the girl who'd been driving. We'd been asked by the doctors not to get hysterical in front of her, to control ourselves. It was so hard to hold back those tears. I wouldn't mind never having to deal with that again. It really sucked. That's the best way I can put it.

"That night, our whole class — about fifty of us — all gathered at one person's house. We ended up having our own little counseling group. We stayed up all night, just talking about Tammy. We reminisced, told stories about how she used to make us laugh or about her smile, all our memories. Whenever someone would cry, I'd be the one to try and comfort that person. In a way it made me feel better. But all the time I was still holding my emotions in. I don't know why, really. I just thought that if I cried, I couldn't help my friends. It would take me almost a year to break down.

"We all went to the funeral. The church overflowed with people. They had to put a TV monitor outside so everyone who wanted to could be part of the service. Lots of kids spoke. I was about to, but I gave my place up to another girl. For her, it was a changing point in her life.

"Over the next few months, my parents wanted to be with me, to help me deal with Tammy's death, but I didn't want to be with them. I hated having to go home, to the thought of being alone in my room, which is adorned with pictures of my friends. The idea of sitting there surrounded by all those photos of happy, healthy Tammy, I couldn't face it. But I would never take the pictures down. To this day, I haven't.

"I know it hurt my parents, but I needed to be with my friends. My friends have always been my life, but during that time they were my lifeline. We were all each other's lifeline. Without each other we wouldn't have made it through. Even with that support, it took so long for it to sink in. Tammy's not on vacation. She's not at some other school. She didn't move away. She's not coming back."

"No, you don't know how I feel."

"People always wonder what they can say at times like this. The answer is nothing — there's nothing you can say, especially not, 'I know how you feel.' I want to smack people who say that. Because they don't know what I feel, just as I don't know what others are feeling. We're all unique, no two human beings feel the same way about anything, especially not about something like this. The best thing anyone said to me was, 'I'm here for you. If you need me, I'm here. You're not going through this alone. I love you.' It's not the words so much as just knowing in your heart that someone is willing to hold you when you cry.

"It's been two years now. My friends and I still talk about Tammy all the time. We'll still see some girl wearing a dress and go, 'Tammy had one just like it — she always wore that color.' Or, 'Yeah, remember when Tammy did that stupid thing,' stuff like that. In that way, Tammy will always be with me.

"Losing one of your best friends changes your life. It has to. Because you suddenly know that things can change at any minute. You need to let people know you love them. I don't believe in fights over stupid things anymore, because your friends could be gone in an instant. What's really eerie is that just before Tammy died, we'd all been fighting, and we'd just all made up, like the day before. On the day she died, I'd given her a big hug and kiss and said, 'I love you. I'll see you tonight.' Tammy died knowing she was loved by her family and her friends. And that helps a little.

"I now know how precious life is. The whole experience has made me more determined than ever to be an activist against drunk driving and against drugs. You can have a fun life without that stuff. I mean, life's pretty cool. Why waste it?"

Nothing endures but change

"Last year, the producers of *7th Heaven* asked how I felt about doing an episode based on what happened to Tammy. At first I said no, because it was too soon. I didn't know how much pain and anguish I'd have to deal with to shoot an episode like that. But eventually I decided to do it. Luckily, Stephen Collins, the actor who plays my dad on the show, directed it. He was really sensitive to me all the way through. A lot of my friends were allowed on the set, and having them there helped, too.

"Even though the fictional story was way different, it felt like it was happening all over again. It was scary, almost like I was losing someone else. Yet it comforted me in a way. When the episode was over, it reminded me that it was over in real life, too.

"The episode was titled 'Nothing Endures But Change.' When I watched the finished show on TV, I was proud of it. It was like I'd conquered a major obstacle in getting over my grief. More importantly, I hoped that episode might help other people — maybe even save someone's life.

"If there's something I would want to say to anyone who's lost a loved one, it's this: Your loved one will never leave you — his or her spirit lives on in you. I didn't lose my friend. Friends are forever."

JEREMY AND JASON LONDON

"NOT A DAY GOES BY THAT I DON'T THINK OF HER."

The London twins Jeremy and Jason are two of the hottest young actors around. Although both have compiled a long line of credits, Jason is probably best known for the flick *Dazed and Confused*. He also has a starring role in the horror sequel *Carrie II*. Jeremy is most familiar to TV viewers as *Party of Five*'s Griffin.

The fact that *either* twin is even *in* showbiz is amazing. No one, least of all the boys, would have ever predicted anything so miraculous happening to them. Growing up, Jason's and Jeremy's lives were as hardscrabble as they come. They were born in San Diego, California, and brought up, along with their younger sister, Dedra, in Oklahoma and Texas. Their parents divorced when the twins were five years old, and all three kids lived with their waitress mom, Debbie. In search of a better life, the little family moved six times in thirteen years. Most of those times they lived in trailer parks.

At first their impoverished circumstances weren't an issue. "We didn't know how poor we were in Oklahoma, because everyone was poor and living in trailers," Jeremy described in *US* magazine.

It was pointed out to them in eighth grade when they moved to DeSoto, Texas, outside of Dallas. Jason said to a reporter, "DeSoto was pretty snobby. The first day I heard some kids making fun of another kid because he was wearing clothes from Wal-Mart. And all the clothes *we* wore were from Wal-Mart. I begged Mom not to send us back to that school."

The lack of material possessions and the constant moving around brought them closer as a family. "We grew up so poor that we had to be close," Jeremy once told *Teen* magazine. "We never really had anything besides ourselves. We never had real nice houses or cars or anything like that. People used to ignore us because we were poor."

Jason added, "You had to be strong and independent. But dealing with hardship helped me confront adversity with more confidence."

Little did he know what kind of adversity was right around the corner.

As teenagers, Jason and Jeremy took what odd jobs they could find to help support the family. One memorable job had catastrophic results; another brought a stroke of luck. On a construction site, teenage Jason had an accident with a forklift that severed two of his toes. And then there was Jeremy's job, waiting tables at a Holiday Inn in DeSoto, Texas, in 1989. A customer happened to be a model and actress. She took one look at Jeremy and made a fateful suggestion: "Go look up my agent in Dallas."

All three Londons — Jason and Jeremy, who were eighteen, and fifteen-year-old Dedra — followed up on the suggestion. They drove to Dallas in the car Jason had been able to buy using the insurance money from his accident.

All three, who'd never acted beyond high school plays, enrolled with the agency and took some drama classes. Within a few weeks, all three nailed acting parts. Jason got a leading role in a movie called *The Man in the Moon*. Jeremy and Dedra nabbed parts in an NBC TV-movie called *In Broad Daylight*. Soon after, both boys appeared in the TV series *I'll Fly Away*, and Jason had just signed to star in another movie. In 1991, the start of a new decade, things were definitely looking up for the London family. In fact, they were sure that the bad times were behind them.

How tragically wrong they were.

"People just take for granted . . . that you'll be there tomorrow."

Jason and Jeremy had relocated to California, but Dedra, a teenage bride and pregnant with her first child, stayed in Texas. Four months after the birth of her son in 1992, she was killed in a car crash.

The twins were devastated. They coped with the horrific tragedy in very different ways. "After Dedra passed away, I was pretty filled with rage," Jason admitted in an interview, adding, "but I feel my Christian faith has helped me get through that."

Jeremy, no less devastated, admitted to *People* magazine, "Not a day goes by that I don't think of her."

The tragedy forced Jeremy — who actually relived that grief when his TV character, Griffin, lost *his* sister a few years later — to reevaluate his life. "I just realized that life is short, and you have to live it to the fullest."

For Jeremy that means, among other things, getting into extreme sports, big time. He goes snowboarding, does motocross, Rollerblades, and plays hockey. He never forgets why. "I play hard," he said in an interview. "I do those things to release anxiety and to keep me feeling young and alive. Too many people close to me have died." Five years after Dedra's death, the twins lost their nineteen-year-old stepbrother, again in a car accident.

As Jeremy said to a reporter, "You have to realize that your life is so important, and you need to love your brothers and sisters and your family. There is so much sibling rivalry in families, and people just take for granted every day that you'll be there tomorrow."

Although both Jason and Jeremy are serious about their acting, neither gets bent out of shape over not getting a particular role or other career-related disappointments. Jeremy noted, "I remind myself that I'm not out there digging with my nails like my parents did. I say, 'You get to act for a living. You're fortunate. So act like it.'"

Jason added in *People* magazine, "We can get low, but we can't get any lower than where we've been."

SEAN "PUFFY" COMBS

"I JUST WANTED TO WAKE UP. I JUST KNEW IT WAS A DREAM."

When you turn on MTV lately, it seems that at least every other video has the Sean "Puffy" Combs stamp on it. The videos are either from his own debut album, *No Way Out*, or from artists the twenty-seven-year-old wonder has produced. Check out the *Billboard* rap, R&B, and pop charts, and at any given time in the last couple of years there were at least three Puffy-connected songs in the top ten! Sean, also known as Puff Daddy, heads up his own record label, Bad Boy Records, and his own production company, Bad Boy Entertainment. He created and funds Daddy's House, a New York City community program that helps homeless kids and kids in the foster-care system. He also owns a restaurant in Manhattan called Justin's, named after his oldest son. In the near future there are plans for Puffy to start his own movie production company, Bad Boy Films, star in a movie, possibly buy the magazine *Notorious*, and start a clothing line called Sean John.

Whether you call him Sean, Puffy, or Puff Daddy, he is a crazy-huge influence in the entertainment world as well as in society in general. Even though he is one of the biggest names in the music industry and one of the most covered personalities in newspapers and magazines, Sean "Puffy" Combs has not been afraid to show his most personal and vulnerable side. Puffy has not been afraid to shed tears for the loss of a best friend. In every action he has taken since the 1997 shooting death of rapper Christopher Wallace, who was better known as the Notorious B.I.G. or Biggie Smalls, Puffy has made it clear that all the fame and fortune in the world will never make up for the loss of a friend.

Little Puffy

Indeed, Puffy is no stranger to personal loss. He was born and grew up in Harlem, New York City. He was close to his mom, Janice, and his dad, Marvin, and he was a big brother to sister Keisha. But when Puffy was three years old, tragedy struck. His father was killed in a street incident near Central Park. Instead of fleeing the city, Puffy told *Rolling Stone*, his mom kept the family in Harlem. "She didn't want to raise me in the suburbs. She wanted me to get the strength from Harlem, the strength of growing up in the city." However, when Puffy was twelve, his mom, who was a teacher, did move the family to the suburb of Mount Vernon. Still, it was just a short train ride to the city, so Puffy had the best of both worlds.

He attended Mount St. Michael's Academy, an all-boys private school. It was at St. Michael's that he earned his nickname Puffy. He was on the school football team, and he had a tendency to puff up his chest to look bigger and more dangerous. From that moment on, he was known as Puffy.

But it wasn't all fun and games for Puffy. As the preteen man of the house, he felt a need to help out with the finances. So when he was twelve, he lied about his age and got a job delivering newspapers. That wasn't enough. Puffy established several other identities so he could have more newspaper routes and make more money. He was preparing for the future, but Puffy told *Teen People* magazine, "I didn't know exactly what I was going to do, but I saw myself making it. Initiative is key. Somebody who wants to be somebody is going to work as hard as they can to fulfill that dream."

Puffy becomes Puff Daddy

In 1988, when Puffy graduated from St. Michael's, he headed to Washington, D.C., to attend prestigious Howard University. Never content to just sit around, Puffy balanced classes with a side business of producing house parties and concerts for the students. In 1990, Washington became too small for Puffy, and he landed an internship at a new independent record label, Uptown Records, in New York City. Juggling his studies at Howard with his duties working with artists like Mary J. Blige, Heavy D., and Jodeci at Uptown, Puffy commuted back and forth between Manhattan and Washington. Eventually he decided to concentrate on the music business and dropped out of Howard. Then, in 1993, Puffy started his own record label, Bad Boys Records, which boasted artists such as 112 and Faith Evans.

When a friend from *The Source* magazine gave Puffy a demo tape of a young rapper from Brooklyn, he was blown away. The artist was Christopher Wallace, an XXXL young man who performed under several stage names, among them Notorious B.I.G. and Biggie Smalls.

"He had so much melody in his voice," Puffy told *Rolling Stone*. "It was like he was rapping, but it was so catchy, it was almost like he was singing. And he was such a clever poet, the way he put his words together, the way he saw things. He saw things so vivid. If you sat and listened to a Biggie Smalls record in the dark, you see a whole movie in front of you. And the amazing thing is, Biggie never wrote down his lyrics. He'd sit and compose them in his head. Beyond that, he had a mysterious side to him. If you was in a room with him, you couldn't stop staring at him. He was just different — the way he looked, the way he walked, the way he talked — the way he rapped."

Puffy knew he wanted to sign Biggie to Bad Boy. At the time, he didn't know that Biggie was going to become his best friend. But after working together 24-7 on Biggie's debut album, *Ready to Die*, the two were totally tight. The album reflected Biggie's unique view of the street life. From the first cut to the last, it painted a picture of the lure of the fast lane, and the eventual personal loss from trying to keep up with it. In many ways, *Ready to Die* reflected the life choices Biggie had to make. Puffy quickly realized that if Biggie hadn't chosen to follow the music, he probably would have been working the streets.

"I want to try to uplift as many people as I can out of that life," Puffy told *Rolling Stone*. "And with [Biggie], I wanted to do it in a way so that he doesn't have to go back — and even more than that, he doesn't *want* to go back — and understands that there's a lot of things that are wrong out there. That's why it was so important [for me] to show him how to become a businessman. This was a big dream for him. He wanted to get out of the street life, and rapping was his way out. In the end, he had become an enterprise — a kid from the streets who didn't even have his diploma. It felt good to see him make something out of himself."

"I ain't got nothing but love for them." — Biggie Smalls

Ready to Die hit the mark. It shot up the charts, and Biggie Smalls, the Notorious B.I.G., became a major voice in rap. In 1997, Puffy was putting the final touches on Biggie's second album, *Life After Death*. Taking a break from the studio, the two decided to go to the Soul Train Awards in Los Angeles. It was a time to celebrate, have some fun. They both believed *Life After Death* was going to be even bigger than *Ready to Die*. That was definitely enough reason for Puffy and Biggie to hit the limelight and enjoy themselves. After the awards show, they went to a party. It was in the wee hours of the morning when they left the festivities, but Biggie was still flying high, anticipating the release of the first single from his album. "I [want them to] know I ain't got nothing but love for them," Puffy remembers Biggie saying as they drifted out to the parking lot with a group of friends. They headed to separate cars. Puffy pulled out of the parking lot before Biggie. He was several cars ahead of Biggie when the first shots rang out in the cold, still night. One of the guys in Puffy's car turned around and saw that Biggie's car had been hit. It was only a matter of seconds before Puffy jumped out of his car and ran to Biggie's. Puffy's best friend was slumped over the steering wheel.

Even though Puffy and another friend, Damien, rushed Biggie to the hospital, it was too late. In his conversation with *Rolling Stone*, Puffy recalls those awful minutes. "I was, like, 'I think he's dead,' I'm saying it inside myself. So we get to the hospital, running lights, everything, and we carry him inside. And we were there for maybe, like, half an hour. Then the doctors come and tell us the news. I was on my knees praying the whole time. I was just stuck. I couldn't understand. It was moving so fast. I just could not believe it was real."

Puffy was devastated. The next day, when he left L.A. to go back to New York, Puffy lost it. "I just did not want to leave him," Puffy continued. "So then I'm about to get on the plane. And I'm seeing the plane pull up, that's when I just break down. I'm about to leave L.A. without my man, you know what I'm saying? He's getting left here — he's at the morgue. I just wanted him to be with me, sitting right there with me, going back to New York. I just wanted to wake up. I just knew it was a dream."

But it wasn't a dream. It was all too real. In the flash of a bullet, Biggie had become another street violence statistic. Back in New York, Puffy didn't find any peace. He could not accept the death of Biggie. Five months later, Puffy admitted to the *Rolling Stone* reporter that it still overwhelmed him. "I try to block that out. . . . I've cried a lot, and I deal with it, but it's, like, the pain don't get less. . . . It's hard to really deal with. It was, like, you know, if I didn't speak to him . . . something was wrong with the day. . . . He just treated you like we were in our own little world, with nobody else. It's just me and you, treating each other good."

"I want to make sure that Biggie's name goes down in history with positivity."

The almost two years since Biggie's death have been a real roller coaster for Puffy. If he allows himself to think about that awful night, Puffy says he still feels the way he did when the doctors came out and told him Biggie had died. But after a while, Puffy realized he had to go on — for his sake, for the sake of his family, friends, Bad Boy artists, and all those others who counted on him. He also had to go on for Biggie's sake.

Puffy took courage from Biggie's mom. "If she ain't going to give up, if she ain't jumping off no bridges — she's having to get up and go to work still, take care of [Biggie's] kids — I've got to get myself together," Puffy explained in his *Rolling Stone* interview.

So it started. For Puffy, going on was working hard with his artists and the music they were putting out. And it meant taking a stand. Puffy was the first to admit that a lot of rap songs were pretty negative. Though they may have expressed a reality about life on the streets, many of them glamorized violence. Some felt the songs set a tone — a dangerous one. Puffy was determined to make changes.

"We going to definitely watch what we say now because we have to take responsibility," Puffy said when discussing lyrics with a reporter from *Spin* magazine. "We can talk and complain about the social climate, but we also have to try to do something about it. I want to make sure that Biggie's name goes down in history with positivity."

And to *Rolling Stone*, he added, "I'm going to make so many records that make you feel good. I just want it to also be known at the end of the day, [Biggie] was instrumental in changing the vibe in the community — not in hip-hop, but in the community. I'm going to try for that."

And Puffy has done just that. One of the first projects he released was the single "I'll Be Missing You." Puffy and Faith Evans (Biggie's ex-wife) recorded this duet as a tribute to the late rapper. The first week it was on the charts, "I'll Be Missing You" was number one, only the fifth song to ever do that. It was probably the most played song of 1997, and every time it played, Puffy's love of his best friend was renewed. But he didn't stop there. Puffy took the money he personally earned from "I'll Be Missing You," three million dollars, and set up a trust fund for Biggie's two kids, Christopher and T'yanna. He wanted to make sure that Biggie's mom would never have to worry about the future of her grandchildren.

But that wasn't enough. Puffy wanted to do more for the community that he and Biggie had come from. "That way I can make his death mean something for him, me, and everybody else," he told *Spin*.

So Puffy took his share of the profits from Biggie's album *Life After Death* to fund community programs such as Daddy's House. There, Puffy told *Teen People*, city kids are offered "positive experiences — computer camps, summer camps, boys' and girls' clubs, ethics classes. . . . I've gotten to where I've gotten because I had a chance to dream, and I want to instill that in kids. All kids have a spark in them. Somebody just needs to ignite that spark. They can accomplish anything."

DREW
BARRYMORE

**"THE NEWS OF MY GRANDPA'S DEATH
TOUCHED ME IN THE ONE PLACE I'D DEEMED
OFF-LIMITS TO EVERYONE: MY HEART."**

Drew Barrymore was born to one of the legendary families of American theater and film. Four years old when she made her movie debut in *Altered States*, Drew was quickly running with Hollywood's biggies. Steven Spielberg himself picked the seven-year-old Drew to play Gertie in *E.T.: The Extraterrestrial*.

Amazingly, Drew also began running with the Hollywood — and New York — fast crowd. At six, she dyed her hair for the first time; at nine she drank champagne at a wrap party for *Firestarter* — and passed out; at ten, Drew was a regular on the celebrity party and club scene. She drank. She smoked. She even admits she had become a pretty good kisser! "I became guy-crazy, an addiction in which I used boys to find love, affirmation, and self-worth," Drew admitted in a 1995 *YM* article. By the time Drew was eleven, she had been introduced to drugs, and the next three years became something of a blur. Drew entered a drug and alcohol rehab when she was fourteen. Unfortunately it was a revolving door since she admitted herself and checked out a number of times before she completed her treatment. When Drew was fifteen, she collaborated with author Todd Gold on her autobiography, *Little Girl Lost*. In it, the teenage Drew explored her strange journey through fame, depression, addiction, and eventual enlightenment. *Little Girl Lost* became a best-seller, and it was the start of Drew reclaiming her talent and her life.

One thing Drew regrets the most about her "dark years" is any disappointment or pain she caused the people who loved her. Perhaps the one person she felt the worst about hurting was her maternal grandfather. When he died unexpectedly, Drew thought she had lost any opportunity of setting things right — until a counselor at the treatment center made a wise suggestion. Read this excerpt from Drew's book and see how she handled her terrible loss.

A letter from Drew's heart

"Hi, Mom," I said.

"Hi," she said in a soft voice, a near whisper really.

"What's wrong?" I asked.

"I have something to tell you."

"What?"

"Well, your grandfather died," she said.

Not even listening to the rest of what she had to say, I burst into tears. A few minutes later I said good-bye and dropped into a chair. My group counselor asked if I was OK, but I couldn't stop crying. I'd been so involved in my own dark, selfish world, I didn't think anything could affect me. But I was wrong. The news of my grandpa's death touched me in the one place I'd deemed off-limits to everyone: my heart.

It ached in a way, in months past, would've had me running out the door for a drink or drugs. Anything to numb the pain rather than face it. But that was out of the question. I was made to confront the situation head on. "Deal with it, Drew," Betty, one of my counselors, urged.

In a group the next day, I took a big risk. I told everyone that, although Grandpa Mako was one of the people I loved most in the world, I worried that the chance to tell him had passed by because I was into my teenage nonsense and rotten drug use. I wasn't being myself. The last time I'd talked to him, but I feared that wasn't enough.

"Then write it out," Betty urged. "Say good-bye to him."

Dear Granddad,

I don't know how to start this letter, because I'm speechless. I can't picture you not in my life anymore. I'll always remember the wonderful times we had together. Like when we'd go feed the animals in your backyard. And that incredible tree house you built me. And how we'd go sit inside it and talk about adult matters. Just being with you always made me feel happy.

I don't know if you'll understand, but for the past several years I've been wrapped up in the teenage scene. Maybe you thought that I treated grandparents as if they were convenient and cool only when bringing me presents. I never thought about you that way. I truly loved you. I'm sorry if I didn't show it.

I just want you to know that you mean a lot to me. I love you. No matter what, you will always be with me. Your soul, our shared memories, and your love will always be in my heart. I love you . . . and good-bye!
Love,
Drew

Dustin Diamond
(Saved By the Bell)

He plays a comic character, Screech, on NBC's long-running Saved By the Bell, but in real life, he had to deal with the death of his older brother.

Freddie Prinze, Jr.

(I Know What You Did Last Summer)

The hot young star was named for his actor/comedian father, who committed suicide shortly after young Freddie was born.

Tim Allen (*Home Improvement*)

"My father died when I was eleven. I remember being very sad as a teenager. The best advice I got is that, time does help when there is tragedy. It's true. Sometimes things are really awful, but something better is right around the corner." [*Jump*]

Shania Twain

The Canadian-born singing star grew up in poverty. Her biggest fear was that her teachers would realize how poor the family was and the state would come in and take her — and her brothers and sisters — away. Things got tragically worse when she turned 21 and her parents were both killed in a head-on collision with a logging truck. Shania had to take over and raise her three younger siblings. "I became very hard for quite a while," she admitted to *Rolling Stone*. "Just nobody could do anything to even remotely hurt me. I was so numb. Nothing penetrated. It was a very difficult time, but boy, oh boy, did I ever get strong."

Lauren Holly
(Dumb and Dumber)

The glamorous actress lost her older brother, who was 14 when he died in a fire.

Prince William and Prince Harry

They've probably suffered the most famous loss in all the world: their mom, of course, was Princess Diana.

Howie Dorough (Backstreet Boys)

On September 14, 1998 — just as we were doing the final edits on this book — Howie Dorough's 37-year-old sister, Caroline Cochran, died of the autoimmune disease lupus. When the Backstreet Boys got the terrible and unexpected news, they immediately canceled a show they were just about to do in Shakopee, Minnesota. Howie flew down to Raleigh, North Carolina, to be with his family. When fans heard about the tragedy, they responded with an inspiring show of sympathy and condolences.

In response to the fans' letters, cards, e-mails, and phone calls, Howie issued the following statement:

"Regarding the recent passing of my sister, Caroline Cochran, the outpouring of emotion and sympathy I have received from the fans and the media has been overwhelming. Caroline was only thirty-seven when she lost her battle with the disease called Lupus. This disease affects the immune system, often striking down young people like my sister in their prime.

"Instead of sending cards or gifts in memory of my sister, I would request that a donation be made to the fund I have established in her name. This donation would help the study of this disease, so that hopefully a cure can be found and no other family will have to suffer a lost such as ours."

"You can send donations to:

"Caroline Cochran–Lupus Fund at Florida Hospital
c/o Florida Hospital Foundation
616 East Rolloins Street, Suite 103
Orlando, FL 32803

"Thank you — Howie D. of the Backstreet Boys."

HANSON

7

MICHELLE KWAN

James Van Der Beek

ISSUES OF DISAPPOINTMENT AND DEFEAT

Dean Cain

DAVID BOREANAZ

Angela Bassett

Ever wanted something so much you could taste it? Okay, not Sony PlayStation, those Steve Madden platforms, or a date with crush du jour. We're talking a long-term goal, something you *know* you have the talent for, something you not only *can* do, but *must* do — something you must be. You want to be an actor? A rock star? An artist? A writer? A pro athlete?

Whatever — you go!

Such is our country's attitude, as all the slogans remind us. "It's a free country, we deserve to be all that we can be."

But what happens when we can't? What happens when, on the way to "You go" we sputter . . . and stall out?

What happens in that mortifying moment when you realize . . . uh-oh . . . you're *not* going to reach that one goal after all? Where do you go from there? Here are the stories of some very successful and popular stars who had to face defeat and learned how to rebound. Each did it in a different way.

Are *you* dealing with defeat right now, facing what you consider personal failure? Check it out: Maybe one of their stories will be an inspiration to you.

HANSON

"RECORD COMPANIES WERE AFRAID TO SIGN US . . ."

Okay, it *is* hard to wrap your brain around the concept that clan Hanson — musicians Isaac, Taylor, and Zachary — traveled a disappointment-strewn road to superstardom. Did they *not* achieve global superstardom before the age of twenty (and, in Zac's case, predating puberty)? Was titling their multi-platinum album *Middle of Nowhere not* a nod to their "overnight" success?

Well, yes and no. Everyone's aware that Hanson hit it big, young. Few, however, know that they took *years* to do it. And fewer still seem to realize the deep disappointments, criticism, skepticism, and setbacks endured along the way.

From 1991 to 1996, no one who could help them in the music industry took them seriously or wanted anything to do with them. They were viewed as simply small-time, a cute little family band with no shot at the big time.

Hanson didn't see it that way at all, though.

"No one ever thought, 'Wow, they're really going places.'"

The dream began when the Hanson family recognized the precocious talent of the three oldest boys. "There was always singing and music around the house," Ike has said. "It was the most natural thing in the world for us to sing together."

Parents Walker and Diana — both amateur musicians, it's worth noting — didn't think it was merely cute that little Ike, Taylor, and Zac could memorize song lyrics so naturally and harmonize so awesomely. The Hanson 'rents didn't find third-grader Ike's amazing ability to compose original tunes merely brag-worthy. They saw more than preternatural talent. They saw the passion the boys had for music and understood the potential. They acted on both.

From the get-go, the family shared and shaped the dream that Isaac, Taylor, and Zac could be huge stars.

They weren't naive. They knew that a whole lot of work, expense, time, and energy would have to be devoted to the cause. With a zeal born of love and deep belief in their brood, they went for it. The goal was to get the boys signed to a major record label.

The quest began in 1991.

Hours each day were spent learning new songs, choreographing routines. As Ike, Tay, and Zac grew, more time went into composing original songs and, eventually, learning to play instruments. The family living room was turned into a studio. Money that was hard to come by was spent on piano lessons.

Putting together an act took away from playtime, TV time, video game time, everything but schooltime. Zac has described, "Instead of doing our chores, we usually spent time writing a new song." Soon rehearsals were up to four hours a day — every day! Yet the boys didn't complain. Making music meant everything.

Hanson started as small as small can be. Their first gigs were at picnics and Christmas parties for the oil company that employed their dad. They advanced — through the dogged promotional efforts of their mom, mostly, who sometimes had to practically beg to let her boys perform — to singing at neighbors' backyard barbecues, elementary school assemblies, Little League baseball games, minor league games, local amusement parks. Everyone who heard them agreed they were great. A friend recalls, "They were invited to sing at my girlfriend's party, and they just came in and blew everyone's minds, these three little kids singing great harmonies."

Kudos abounded, but cash was in short supply. Mostly, they didn't even get paid. But they kept at it, finding other means of compensation. Hanson spent their own money to design and produce T-shirts, which they'd sell at their local concerts. They devised mailing lists of young fans and dug into the family coffers to send out announcements to each and every one about upcoming gigs. That's how they built an audience.

Their hometown, Tulsa, is host to an annual music fair called Mayfest. While up-and-coming performers dominate the main stages at Mayfest, there was also a community stage reserved for hometown acts not destined for stardom. As one observer put it, "The community stage was for anyone who wanted to play. No talent was required. People who would play the community stage at Mayfest would play for free at a car wreck."

As if *that* weren't humiliating enough, the first year Hanson played — 1992 — they were part of a contest for best local act. After a fifteen-song set in which they poured their hearts out, they lost.

Dispiriting as that must have been, worse, it reflected the opinions of music journalists in the Southwest. As one put it, "No one thought of them as a professional band. They were just the little

Hanson brothers who'd show up at Mayfest and sing at a church or two, that's it. The reaction to them was, 'Oh, aren't they cute? Their harmonies are fantastic, and they really sound good, but so what?' No one ever thought, 'Wow, they're really going places.'"

"Can we sing for you?"

The Hanson family was, of course, going places — literally. They traveled to gigs all over the Southwest in their own rickety van, which was prone to breakdowns.

When none of their efforts to attract a record label talent scout panned out, they rented studio time and paid for professional backup musicians to record an independent CD, *Boomerang*.

They sent it around to record companies all over the United States. Not one responded positively. Rejections ruled. By this time, most people would have given up — at least temporarily. The boys were still young, and there were others at home to be cared for. Chasing the dream of stardom could wait.

Or not. Instead of giving up, the boys tried to figure out what was wrong. Taylor had a theory: "Record companies were afraid to sign us [on the basis of *Boomerang*] because we were white kids doing R&B music, and it didn't exactly work."

So Hanson went back to the drawing board and started all over again, refining their sound. Their second, independently produced CD was called *MMMBop*, and it had more pop flavor. Still, it got them exactly nowhere.

By 1995, the Hanson family knew they needed professional management. But of course, no one was taking them seriously.

South by Southwest is an annual music confab that takes place in Austin, Texas. Traditionally, unsigned bands and record company talent scouts come together in hopes of hooking up. Unlike most bands who come to South by Southwest, Hanson was not officially booked to play anywhere — that's how small-time they were.

Undeterred, the trio simply set themselves up and played on random street corners, hoping to snag the attention of *anyone* in the music biz who would help them. "We were doing our little song and dance, with a boom box behind us," Taylor recalls. No wonder no one cared.

Still, the boys were never too proud or too despondent to plow on. When music manager Chris Sabec was pointed out to them, they simply tapped him on the shoulder and asked hopefully, "Can we sing for you?"

Chris, who ended up signing the brothers, remembers the incident well. "I was having lunch when the boys came up and asked if they could sing for me. Everyone else was ignoring them."

The road to stardom remained rocky. Chris has revealed, "Most record labels advised me to get away from this act as fast as possible. People said [representing Hanson] would ruin and humiliate me. It was very difficult."

Ike, Tay, and Zac continued to polish their act, compose more tunes — by 1996, they had more than a hundred to their credit — record demo tapes, and with Chris's help, send them to record companies. The rejection slips they received could have papered a small room.

It took until May 1996 for the band to convince one talent scout from one record company — which had rejected them in the past! — to come see them perform at a county fair in Kansas. And that made all the difference.

For it took one person with the power to sign them to take a chance — and finally, after five years of struggle, the impossible dream was realized. Isaac, Taylor, and Zac got signed to Mercury Records. And the rest is Han-story.

The moral of the story? Never give up.

MICHELLE KWAN

"THE ONLY BAD THING ABOUT WINNING IS THAT SOMEDAY YOU HAVE TO LOSE WHAT YOU'VE WON."

Michelle Kwan, eighteen, is the youngest child of Estella and Danny Kwan. The future ice-skating champion grew up with her older brother, Ron, and older sister, Karen, in southern California. Ron got interested in ice hockey, and then Karen followed him to the rink, but as an ice-skater. Little Michelle followed suit. In ice-skating, she found her joy. And when she watched Brian Boitano win the gold at the 1988 Winter Olympics, Michelle vowed that one day she would compete at the ultimate sports event, too. Soon she and Karen were working with a coach and competing in amateur events. When Michelle and Karen were both accepted as students at the prestigious Ice Castle rink in Lake Arrowhead, they were on their way to the top. Michelle excelled and began making a name for herself, first on the juniors level and then on the seniors.

In 1996 Michelle Kwan won the gold medal at the Nationals. It was her fourth time at the Nationals, but she admits it was the first time she felt she was equal with the other skaters. She felt confident. And she won.

Nothing was better than that feeling. She was on the way to fulfilling all her dreams. What Michelle didn't know was that the road to the ultimate success isn't always as smooth as the ice she skated on. In her autobiography, *Michelle Kwan, My Story, Heart of a Champion*, she shares how she learned, through success and defeat, the true meaning of a winner.

Now that I'd reached the top, the requests for interviews and appearances went through the roof. . . . I was invited to every skating exhibition. People wanted me to make special appearances all over the place. I did all kinds of TV shows. I was even invited to visit President Clinton in the White House. I would have loved to have gone, but I didn't have enough time! "Sorry, Mr. President. Can't make it."

I got thousands of fan letters and autograph requests. Kids sent me presents. . . . It was so sweet! I always wrote back and sent a picture. I couldn't believe how nice all the fans were.

At Ice Castle, my friends didn't act differently toward me. But whenever new young skaters came to the rink, I'd see them pointing at me and hear them saying in a whisper, "That's Michelle Kwan." They looked up to me the way I had looked up to Lu Chen, Nancy Kerrigan, and Kristi Yamaguchi when I was little. It was really neat to think I might inspire a new young skater.

When I told people that I wasn't really surprised to become world champion, the answer maybe sounded a little arrogant. But the fact was that I wasn't surprised. That's not the word for it. Excited, overwhelmed, happy: yes. But ever since I was seven, I had imagined myself as a championship skater.

Whenever I'd ask myself, Can this really happen to me? an inner voice had always answered *yes*. I'd been working for it my whole life. So *surprise* is not really the right word.

And when the day came for me to lose it, I wouldn't be surprised then, either. Right now, I was the youngest American world champion ever and the third-youngest world champion period. I felt incredibly lucky to have achieved so much at such a young age.

After I won, everything was happening so fast that it made my head spin. I began to wonder if I'd ever have a chance to enjoy it. My dad always says, "There's a good and a bad side to everything in life." The only bad thing about winning is that someday you have to lose what you've won. I already knew I couldn't be world champion forever. I just wished I could stop everything and look at it all, as if it were a picture, so I could appreciate what had happened.

When I look back on my life, I have to say that the long process of *becoming* world champion was the most fun I've had. Every time I stepped on the ice, I was so excited that I never thought of fear. I loved to skate — to feel like I was flying. It seemed that there was nowhere to go but up.

But *being* world champ? Wow. That was something else altogether. I was standing up there with a gold medal, and the view was great. There was only one problem: Where do you fly from there?

The summer after Michelle's championship season, she went on the Tom Collins Campbell's Soups Tour.

Most skaters use programs on tour that aren't as challenging as their regular long programs. But not all. Brian Boitano, for one, is amazing. He goes out there each night and puts every ounce of himself into his program. You can see that for him skating itself is the greatest thrill and the highest honor — greater and higher than all the medals he has won.

I wanted to skate all-out like that, too. I knew I couldn't let up just because I had a couple of gold medals. I had just won Worlds, but I was already thinking about the next season. What were my new goals? The answer was fuzzy . . . not to lose? What kind of goal was that?

I decided that the thing to do was simply to work harder than I'd ever worked before. To not let up for a minute. "Work *harder*, be yourself, and have fun" was my new motto.

It should have been my happiest summer, but I was feeling confused about my goals. *Keeping* the championship was my new objective, not getting it. Suddenly I felt more serious than I had before. Having fun got to be hard.

After the summer tour, Michelle returned home for the skating season break. But soon she was gearing up for the 1996–1997 season and found she wasn't feeling happy.

Practice wasn't going so well, either. My new skates were a nightmare. Dad made the heels lower, then higher. The blades were messed up, too. When I wanted to go one way, they'd go the other. We were spending hours a day working on my new program, and my feet were killing me.

I was not happy.

So I went back, and I said, "Dad, can you please tell me what my problems are now?"

Well, this time he didn't even have to think. He came up with so many answers that I needed a pen and paper to write them down. I almost wanted to say, "Sorry I asked."

First on his list was *appreciation*. Dad said I needed to appreciate my life more. The next thing on Dad's list was *perspective*. I had lost my perspective on the sport. Where did it fit into the *big* picture of my life — the picture of me, not only as a skater, but as a *person*? Had I forgotten that skating wasn't all of life?

Throughout the year, the list kept growing. I knew he was right, but I didn't know how to fix my problems. And he couldn't tell me. No one could. The only solution I could come up with was *work*. So, I buckled down and worked harder than ever.

In the days leading up to the 1997 Nationals in Nashville, Tennessee, reporters asked me how I was dealing with the pressure of being a defending champion. I'd won six gold medals since San Jose. People were saying I couldn't be beat. How did I do it? they asked.

I thought about my motto and the things my mom and dad had always told me. . . . I told those reporters, with a big smile, "Well, I try to go out there and have fun. I try to remember that it's just a sport. It isn't everything. It's fun." That's just about what I said . . . on national television in front of millions of people.

Then I skated. My short program went well, and I was in first place going into the freeskate. But very few people saw the short program on TV. Millions, on the other hand, saw the freeskate.

That's when it happened. I fell once, then again, and then again. . . . Aaugh! I won't go over it all again.

My dad was right. I had lost perspective. I wasn't skating for the reason I always had — to have fun and fly free. Instead, I was skating not to lose. How had I done this? How had I let the anticipation of this night — this one competition — grow and grow out of proportion, all year long? That wasn't like me at all.

After my program, the world did not see a girl who had just had fun. They saw a girl who was weeping. And this time, not from joy. I was confused and mad at myself, and so disappointed.

. . . All of these things confirmed what I knew that night in Nashville. I knew the answer right away when my dad asked me, "Well, Michelle, what did you learn from this?"

It all clicked into place. I learned that I needed to love the sport again. That's what my dad meant by appreciation and perspective. I needed to love skating for what it was.

I needed to get back to the feeling I'd had before I was world champion. In a way, I needed to become that little kid I'd left behind in Birmingham again. The kid who didn't win any medals at all, but who felt like she had it all. Because she could really *skate*.

It was important for Michelle to regain that spirit as she headed toward the 1997 World Championships in Lausanne, Switzerland.

Sometimes the biggest test of a skater or any athlete is the moment after she falls. Can she find the spirit and the guts to get up and go on? I planned to do all those things in March at the Worlds. . . . I wouldn't be afraid. I would try to skate free.

The media in Lausanne had set up the competition as a duel between Tara Lipinski and me. I was the veteran (at sixteen!), the "artistic" skater. Tara was the wonder kid, the amazing jumping bean who couldn't fall. She was the "technical" skater.

But all skaters know that you have to be strong in both areas if you want to be a champion. And I for one had to compete with myself before I could even think about Tara.

I went into the short program with the highest hopes and the most positive attitude I could find. I did fine . . . until I stepped out on one jump and stumbled on the landing.

I was so mad at myself when it was over. I was crying already. I started picturing myself in my long program — falling just as I had at Nationals.

In the middle of the Worlds, Michelle was told that skating coach Carlo Fassi, whom she had known from Ice Castle, had died suddenly. Then it was announced that Michelle's idol, Scott Hamilton, had been diagnosed with cancer. Once again the word perspective *occurred to Michelle.*

What had I been thinking? Skating isn't a matter of life and death.

I skated second to last in the long program. I glided out to the middle of the rink and took my opening pose. I knew that people were already holding their breath, wondering if I would fall apart like at Nationals.

I made one small mistake, where I turned a triple into a double. But I kept telling myself, like Brian said, just stand up straight and everything will be fine. And it was. Every jump was clean. Every spin was centered.

When it was over, although I'd won the freeskate, my mistake in the short program had cost me. Tara won, and I came in second overall. But that was fine. My wings were back. Not a single tear fell. Some people said I was the happiest silver medalist they'd ever seen. They were right.

In February 1998, Michelle fulfilled a childhood wish — she repre-sented her country at the Olympics in Nagano, Japan. Michelle glided through her programs and when she finished her final performance, she was very happy.

My scores weren't as good as at Nationals. . . . The judges left room for someone to pass me. I knew that. But at that moment only the skating itself mattered. I'd come to the Olympics prepared to skate my best, and I did it. There was nothing to regret about my performance that night.

. . . Tara Lipinski skated second to last. As soon as I heard her scores, I knew that she'd won the gold. It didn't feel okay. I had it, I thought, but it got away.

But once I heard the national anthem during the medal ceremony and started to sing along, things began to make sense. . . . It was a beautiful moment, silver or gold.

What is a champion? To me, a champion isn't someone who never loses or falls down. It's someone who gets back up. Someone who has heart.

And what is a gold medal? I'd never really thought about it before Nagano. But now I realize that it's a dream to strive for. I love my silver medal, because it stands for all my dreams and all I'm still capable of fulfilling.

DAVID BOREANAZ

"I REALIZED FOOTBALL WASN'T GOING TO BE A CAREER FOR ME."

Another popular prime-time TVer might own the name, but no show — or its audience — has *really* been "touched by an Angel" more than *Buffy the Vampire Slayer*. This otherworldly being is the hunky and mysterious, brooding and tortured Angel, totally the first 242-year-old sex symbol TV has ever had. He is the on-again, off-again light of the Buffster's life. Okay, so he can't actually be *seen* in any kind of natural light. Because he's a vampire. And their love is pretty well doomed, because, well, she's a vampire slayer. Whatever.

Angel, as brought to life by TV newcomer David Boreanaz, had a major impact the minute he stepped out of the shadows and onto the screen. At first, the character was not even a regular on the show. David, whose only previous TV credit was a one-time bit on *Married . . . With Children* was only hired for a few of the first season's episodes. An instant outpouring of fan affection changed that. Producers could not ignore all the fan mail, the cybershrines —

including the famous Angel's Shrine of Drool — and quickly ramped the boy up to full costar status.

It gets better. Just after two seasons of *Buffy* had aired came an announcement: The character will spin off and star in his *own* TV show, *Angel*, to start airing in the fall of 1999. David Boreanaz headlines.

Cool, right? Cooler still when you consider that acting was but a fallback position for David. He only settled on it when the one dream he'd had all through his childhood went bust.

"I was obsessed . . . with [football]."

David grew up in Philadelphia, Pennsylvania, with his parents and two older sisters. From the get-go, the kid was a sports natural, practically to the gridiron born. He ate, slept, and dreamed football, watched games on TV, attended pro games — and played it, too. He started in Peewee League in elementary school and played every year on every school and town team. He dreamed of going pro, and he certainly showed talent. As David admitted to *Twist* magazine, "I was obsessed with it, it was all I wanted to do."

He did more than practice. To get himself in shape, "I drank tons of milk and ate green beans because I heard that made you run faster and jump higher," David divulged to a reporter.

It seemed to work. He attended the exclusive Malvern Prep High School and played on the varsity team. His positions were wide receiver and defense back.

In most high schools, top athletes are usually among the popular crowd. That was true at David's school, too. Being a varsity football player gave him cachet, a cool identity. It helped, too, that he was the son of a local TV star. His dad, Dave Roberts, was a well-known TV weathercaster in Philadelphia. David joked in *Seventeen* magazine, "In high school, the football players would razz me if it rained, like my dad made it rain on purpose."

In fact, for his first three years in high school, David was totally part of the in crowd. Aside from varsity football, he was secretary of the student council. Plus he played other sports — he didn't know that one would be his undoing. For David not only ran on the track team, he also did high jumps. In his junior year, during one of those high jumps, he injured his left knee. The injury was severe enough to keep him off the gridiron, pretty much for good. "I realized that football wasn't going to be a career for me," he told *Twist* magazine.

"It was a trying period for me."

Things seemed to get more confusing after that. It wasn't only that his dream was gone in a cloud of smoke. Physically and socially he began to feel more awkward than awesome. "It was a trying period for me," he once revealed. "You know, you have all these hormones racing inside of you. You don't know where you're going. You're stepping left when you should be stepping right. Things are growing on you that you haven't seen growing there before. It's embarrassing, it's frightening."

One of David's most embarrassing moments happened on a high school date. "I went to the bathroom and realized I had this huge rip right in the seat of my pants!" David admits to using cover-up tactics for doofy behavior around girls. "I'd bail myself out by doing something totally physical and stupid. I'd spill a glass of water, get up from the table, and take the tablecloth with me. I'd go for any cheap laugh to break the tension."

"I'm not going to be miserable in a miserable situation."

In the midst of all the tension, the sudden confusion about who was he, if not a jock, and who would he be, if not a pro football star, David turned to his family for support. Years earlier, his dad had given him self-help books. David explained in an on-line interview, "My father gave me the books for inspiration."

Eventually, David came to a decision, which he explained in a *TV Guide* on-line interview. "I'm not going to be miserable in a miserable situation. [Instead, I'll try to figure out] how can I turn this around? Because why hurt myself even more? I mean, there are times when you feel, like, yeah, this is the pits, man. This is terrible. And you get depressed. And then you [have to] just remind yourself that [everything] is temporary. And then you just [go] on and make the best of it."

For David, that meant forgetting football and going on to the next best thing. He took his own advice, and instead of brooding about the career that wasn't to be, he turned to his second passion, the one he felt just as strongly about, but had kept hidden: acting.

"I was seven years old when my parents took me to see a live performance of *The King and I*, starring Yul Brynner," David has related. "I was inspired by Yul Brynner's performance. The show blew me away. That's why I knew I wanted to be an actor. Right after that, I just wanted to see plays and musicals." Luckily, his parents took him all the time.

Why did he feel the need to keep his nascent love for acting under wraps? David has no real answer to that. "I just would never tell anyone," he admitted. "It was weird. When I'd hit the field, it was football. But behind closed doors, it was theater."

Theater became not only his passion, it became his major at college. And after a lot of disappointing, dues-paying years, it paid off. It led to the footlights of the stage, and then the Angel of the night-lights, and now, the spotlight.

He feels incredibly fortunate, grateful to everyone who supported him — fans, friends, and family — and he's never looked back. Not even for a peek.

ISSUES OF DISAPPOINTMENT AND DEFEAT

James Van Der Beek

That Dawson dude was a sports fanatic who wanted to follow in his dad's footsteps [he was a minor league baseball player] and go pro. The concussion he suffered in eighth grade dashed that dream.
On the road to recovery he discovered acting.

Dean Cain
(Superman – The New Adventures)

TV's *Superman* spent his entire life working toward one goal: to be a pro football player. After a stellar, record-breaking career in college football [he played for Princeton], he was drafted by the Buffalo Bills. He never got to play a single game. In training camp, he suffered a knee injury, bad enough to bench his dream forever.

Angela Bassett
(Waiting to Exhale)

"When you're young, I think it's really important to follow that voice in your head that says, "Just try it." If it doesn't work out, at least you followed your dream. Then, you can always follow someone else's dream— but at least follow yours first."
[Jump]